THE RITE OF CONFIRMATION

*A people's booklet
with
official text*

THE LITURGICAL PRESS
Collegeville   Minnesota

Nihil obstat: Robert C. Harren, J.C.L., *Censor deputatus. Imprimatur*: ✠ George H. Speltz, D.D., Bishop of St. Cloud, November 22, 1982.

Liturgical texts released by the National Conference of Bishops of the United States of America and published by authority of the Bishops' Committee on the Liturgy are reproduced in this booklet.

New English translations of the Order of Mass and of the rite of Confirmation, and the translations of the titles, responsorial antiphons, and summaries of the Readings copyright © 1969, 1971, 1974, 1975 International Committee on English in the Liturgy, Inc. All rights reserved.

Scripture texts from *The New American Bible*, © 1970 by the Confraternity of Christian Doctrine are used herein by license of said copyright owner. All rights reserved.

Copyright © 1983, 1986 The Order of St. Benedict, Inc., Collegeville, Minnesota. Printed in the United States of America.

All rights reserved under United States copyright law, and the International and Pan-American Conventions, including the right to reproduce this booklet, or parts thereof, in any form, by mimeograph, or other mechanical or electronic devices.

ISBN 0-8146-1492-2

APOSTOLIC CONSTITUTION
ON THE
SACRAMENT OF CONFIRMATION

PAUL, BISHOP

Servant of the Servants of God
For an Everlasting Memorial

The sharing in the divine nature received through the grace of Christ bears a certain likeness to the origin, development, and nourishing of natural life. The faithful are born anew by baptism, strengthened by the sacrament of confirmation, and finally are sustained by the food of eternal life in the eucharist. By means of these sacraments of Christian initiation, they thus receive in increasing measure the treasures of divine life and advance toward the perfection of charity. It has rightly been written: "The body is washed, that the soul may be cleansed; the body is anointed, that the soul may be consecrated; the body is signed, that the soul too may be fortified; the body is overshadowed by the laying on of hands, that the soul may be enlightened by the Spirit; the body is fed on the body and blood of Christ, that the soul may be richly nourished by God."

Conscious of its pastoral charge, the Second Vatican Ecumenical Council devoted special attention to these sacraments of initiation. It prescribed that the rites should be revised in a way that would make them more suited to the understanding of the faithful. Since the *Rite of Baptism for Children,* revised at the mandate of the Council and published at our command, is already in use, it is now fitting to publish a rite of confirmation, in order to show the unity of Christian initiation in its true light.

In fact, careful attention and application have been devoted in these last years to the task of revising the manner of celebrating this sacrament. The aim of this work has been that "the intimate connection of this sacrament with the whole of Christian initiation may stand out more clearly." But the link between confirmation and the other sacraments of initiation is more easily perceived not simply from the fact that their rites have been more closely conjoined; the rite and words by which confirmation is conferred also make this link clear. As a result the rite and words of this sacrament "express more clearly the holy things they signify and the Christian people, as far as possible, are able to understand them with ease and take part in them fully, actively, and as befits a community."

For that purpose, it has been our wish also to include in this revision what concerns the very essence of the rite of confirmation, through which the faithful receive the Holy Spirit as Gift.

The New Testament shows how the Holy Spirit was with Christ to bring the Messiah's mission to fulfillment. On receiving the baptism of John, Jesus saw the Spirit descending on him (see Mk 1:10) and remaining with him (see Jn 1:32). He was led by the Spirit to undertake his public ministry as the Messiah, relying on the Spirit's presence and assistance. Teaching the people of Nazareth, he showed by what he said that the words of Isaiah, "The Spirit of the Lord is upon me," referred to himself (see Lk 4:17-21).

He later promised his disciples that the Holy Spirit would help them also to bear fearless witness to their faith even before persecutors (see Lk 12:12). The day before he suffered, he assured his apostles that he would send the Spirit of truth from his Father (see Jn 15:26) to stay with them "for ever" (Jn 14:16) and help them to be his witnesses (see Jn 15:26). Finally, after his resurrection, Christ promised the coming descent of the Holy Spirit: "You will receive power when the Holy Spirit comes upon you; then you are to be my witnesses" (Acts 1:8; see Lk 24:49).

On the feast of Pentecost, the Holy Spirit did indeed come down in an extraordinary way on the apostles as they were gathered together with Mary the mother of Jesus and the group of disciples. They were so "filled with" the Holy Spirit (Acts 2:4) that by divine inspiration they began to proclaim "the mighty works of God." Peter regarded the Spirit who had thus come down upon the apostles as the gift of the Messianic age (see Acts 2:17-18). Then those who believed the apostles' preaching were baptized and they too received "the gift of the Holy Spirit" (Acts 2:38). From that time on the apostles, in fulfillment of Christ's wish, imparted to the newly baptized by the laying on of hands the gift of the Spirit that completes the grace of baptism. This is why the Letter to the Hebrews listed among the first elements of Christian instruction the teaching about baptism and the laying on of hands (Heb 6:2). This laying on of hands is rightly recognized by reason of Catholic tradition as the beginning of the sacrament of confirmation, which in a certain way perpetuates the grace of Pentecost in the Church.

This makes clear the specific importance of confirmation for sacramental initiation, by which the faithful "as members of the living Christ are incorporated into him and configured to him through baptism and through confirmation and the eucharist." In baptism, the newly baptized receive forgiveness of sins, adoption as children of God, and the character of Christ by which they are made members of the Church and for the first time become sharers in the priesthood of their Savior (see 1 Pt 2:5, 9). Through the sacrament of confirmation those who have been born anew in baptism receive the inexpressible Gift, the Holy Spirit himself, by whom "they are endowed . . . with special strength." Moreover, having been signed with the character of this sacrament, they are "more closely bound to the Church" and "they are more strictly obliged to spread and defend the faith, both by word and by deed, as true witnesses of Christ." Finally, confirmation is so closely linked with the holy eucharist that the faithful, after being signed by baptism and confirmation, are incorporated fully into the Body of Christ by participation in the eucharist.

From ancient times the conferring of the gift of the Holy Spirit has been carried out in the Church through various rites. These rites have undergone many changes in the East and the West, but always keeping as their meaning the conferring of the Holy Spirit.

In many Eastern rites it seems that from early times a rite of chrismation, not yet clearly distinguished from baptism, prevailed for the conferring of the Holy Spirit. That rite continues in use today in the greater part of the Churches of the East.

In the West there are very ancient witnesses concerning the part of Christian initiation that was later distinctly recognized to be the sacrament of confirmation. There are directives for the performance of many rites after the baptismal washing and before the eucharistic meal — for example, anointing, the laying on of the hand, consignation — contained both in liturgical documents and in many testimonies of the Fathers. Consequently, in the course of the centuries, problems and doubts arose as to what belonged with certainty to the essence of the rite of confirmation. Worth mentioning, however, are at least some of the elements that, from the thirteenth century onward, in the ecumenical councils and in papal documents, cast considerable light on the importance of anointing, but at the same time did not allow the laying on of hands to be forgotten.

Our predecessor Innocent III wrote: "The anointing of the forehead with chrism signifies the laying on of the hand, the other name for which is confirmation, since through it the Holy Spirit is given for growth and strength." Another of our predecessors, Innocent IV, mentions that the apostles conferred the Holy Spirit "through the laying on of the hand, which confirmation or the anointing of the forehead with chrism represents." In the profession of faith of Emperor Michael Palaeologus read at the Council of Lyons II mention is made of the sacrament of confirmation, which "bishops confer by the laying on of hands, anointing with chrism those who have been baptized." The Decree for the Armenians, issued by the Council of Florence, declares that the "matter" of the sacrament of confirmation is "chrism made of olive oil . . . and balsam" and, quoting the words of the Acts of the Apostles concerning Peter and John, who gave the Holy

Spirit through the laying on of hands (see Acts 8:17), it adds: "in the Church in place of that laying on of the hand, confirmation is given." The Council of Trent, though it had no intention of defining the essential rite of confirmation, designated it simply by the term "the holy chrism of confirmation." Benedict XIV made this declaration: "Therefore let this be said, which is beyond dispute: in the Latin Church the sacrament of confirmation is conferred by using sacred chrism or olive oil mixed with balsam and blessed by the bishop, and by the sacramental minister's tracing the sign of the cross on the forehead of the recipient, while the same minister pronounces the words of the form."

Taking account of these declarations and traditions, many theologians maintained that for valid administration of confirmation only the anointing with chrism, done by placing the hand on the forehead, was required. Nevertheless, in the rites of the Latin Church a laying of hands on those to be confirmed prior to anointing them with chrism was always prescribed.

With regard to the words of the rite by which the Holy Spirit is given, it should be noted that already in the primitive Church Peter and John, in order to complete the initiation of those baptized in Samaria, prayed that they might receive the Holy Spirit and then laid hands on them (see Acts 8:15-17). In the East the first traces of the expression *seal of the gift of the Holy Spirit* appeared in the fourth and fifth centuries. The expression was quickly accepted by the Church of Constantinople and still is in use in Byzantine-Rite Churches.

In the West, however, the words of the rite that completes baptism were less settled until the twelfth and thirteenth centuries. But in the twelfth-century Roman Pontifical the formulary that later became the common one first occurs: "I sign you with the sign of the cross and confirm you with the chrism of salvation. In the name of the Father and of the Son and of the Holy Spirit."

From what we have recalled, it is clear that in the administration of confirmation in the East and West, though in different ways, the most important place was occupied by the anointing, which in a certain way represents the apostolic laying on of hands. Since this anointing with chrism is an apt sign of the spiritual anointing of the Holy Spirit who is given to the faithful, we wish to confirm its existence and importance.

As regards the words pronounced in confirmation, we have examined with the consideration it deserves the dignity of the respected formulary used in the Latin Church, but we judge preferable the very ancient formulary belonging to the Byzantine Rite. This expresses the Gift of the Holy Spirit himself and calls to mind the outpouring of the Spirit on the day of Pentecost (see Acts 2:1-4, 38). We therefore adopt this formulary, rendering it almost word for word.

Therefore, in order that the revision of the rite of confirmation may, as is fitting, include even the essence of the sacramental rite, by our supreme apostolic authority we decree and lay down that in the Latin Church the following are to be observed for the future.

THE SACRAMENT OF CONFIRMATION IS CONFERRED THROUGH THE ANOINTING WITH CHRISM ON THE FOREHEAD, WHICH IS DONE BY THE LAYING ON OF THE HAND, AND THROUGH THE WORDS: BE SEALED WITH THE GIFT OF THE HOLY SPIRIT.*

But the laying of hands on the elect, carried out with the prescribed prayer before the anointing, is still to be regarded as very important, even if it is not of the essence of the sacramental rite: it contributes to the complete perfection of the rite and to a more thorough understanding of the sacrament. It is evident that this prior laying on of hands differs from the later laying on of the hand in the anointing of the forehead.

Having established and declared all these elements concerning the essential rite of the sacrament of confirmation, we also approve by our apostolic authority the rite for the same sacrament. This has been revised by the Congregation for Divine Worship, after consultation with the Congregations for the Doctrine of the Faith, for the Discipline

---

*Latin: ACCIPE SIGNACULUM DONI SPIRITUS SANCTI.

of the Sacraments, and for the Evangelization of Peoples on the matters that are within their competence. The Latin edition of the rite containing the new sacramental form will come into effect as soon as it is published; the editions in the vernacular languages, prepared by the conferences of bishops and confirmed by the Apostolic See, will come into effect on the date to be laid down by each conference. The old rite may be used until the end of the year 1972. From 1 January 1973, however, only the new rite is to be used by those concerned.

We intend that everything that we have laid down and prescribed should be firm and effective in the Latin Church, notwithstanding, where relevant, the apostolic constitutions and ordinances issued by our predecessors, and other prescriptions, even those worthy of special mention.

Given in Rome, at Saint Peter's on the fifteenth day of August, the Solemnity of the Assumption of the Blessed Virgin Mary, in the year 1971, the ninth of our pontificate.

Paul PP. VI

INTRODUCTION TO THE RITE OF CONFIRMATION

(Issued August 22, 1971)

I. DIGNITY OF CONFIRMATION

1. Those who have been baptized continue on the path of Christian initiation through the sacrament of confirmation. In this sacrament they receive the Holy Spirit whom the Lord sent upon the apostles on Pentecost.

2. This giving of the Holy Spirit conforms believers more fully to Christ and strengthens them so that they may bear witness to Christ for the building up of his Body in faith and love. They are so marked with the character or seal of the Lord that the sacrament of confirmation cannot be repeated.

II. OFFICES AND MINISTRIES IN THE CELEBRATION OF CONFIRMATION

3. One of the highest responsibilities of the people of God is to prepare the baptized for confirmation. Pastors have the special responsibility to see that all the baptized reach the completion of Christian initiation and therefore that they are carefully prepared for confirmation.

Adult catechumens who are to be confirmed immediately after baptism have the help of the Christian community and, in particular, the formation that is given to them during the catechumenate. Catechists, sponsors, and members of the local Church participate in the catechumenate by means of catechesis and community celebrations of the rites of initiation. For those who were baptized in infancy and are confirmed only as adults the plan for the catechumenate is used with appropriate adaptations.

The initiation of children into the sacramental life is ordinarily the responsibility and concern of Christian parents. They are to form and gradually increase a spirit of faith in the children and, at times with the help of catechism classes, prepare them for the fruitful reception of the sacraments of confirmation and the eucharist. The role of the parents is also expressed by their active participation in the celebration of the sacraments.

4. Pains should be taken to give the liturgical service the festive

and solemn character that its significance for the local Church requires. This will be achieved above all if the candidates are gathered together for a community celebration of the rites. All the people of God, represented by the families and friends of the candidates and by members of the local community, will be invited to take part in such a celebration and will endeavor to express their faith by means of the effects the Holy Spirit has produced in them.

5. As a rule there should be a sponsor for each of those to be confirmed. These sponsors bring the candidates to receive the sacrament, present them to the minister for the anointing, and will later help them to fulfill their baptismal promises faithfully under the influence of the Holy Spirit whom they have received.

In view of contemporary pastoral circumstances, it is desirable that the godparent at baptism, if available, also be the sponsor at confirmation. This change expresses more clearly the link between baptism and confirmation and also makes the function and responsibility of the sponsor more effective.

Nonetheless the option of choosing a special sponsor for confirmation is not excluded. Even the parents themselves may present their children for confirmation. It is for the local Ordinary to determine diocesan practice in the light of local conditions and circumstances.

6. Pastors will see that the sponsors, chosen by the candidates or their families, are spiritually fit to take on this responsibility and have these qualities:

    a. sufficient maturity to fulfill their function;

    b. membership in the Catholic Church and their own reception of Christian initiation through baptism, confirmation, and eucharist;

    c. freedom from any impediment of law to their fulfilling the office of sponsor.

7. The ordinary minister of confirmation is the bishop. Normally a bishop administers the sacrament so that there will be a clearer reference to the first pouring forth of the Holy Spirit on Pentecost: after the apostles were filled with the Holy Spirit, they themselves gave the Spirit to the faithful through the laying on of hands. Thus the reception of the Spirit through the ministry of the bishop shows the close bond that joins the confirmed to the Church and the mandate received from Christ to bear witness to him before all.

The law gives the faculty to confirm to the following besides the bishop:

    a. territorial prelates and territorial abbots, vicars and prefects apostolic, apostolic administrators and diocesan administrators, within the limits of their territory and while they hold office;

    b. in consideration of the person to be confirmed, priests who, in virtue of an office or the mandate of the diocesan bishop, baptize a person who is no longer an infant or receive a person who is already baptized into the full communion of the Catholic Church;

c. in consideration of those who are in danger of death, a pastor or in fact any priest.

8. The diocesan bishop is to administer confirmation himself or to ensure that it is administered by another bishop. But if necessity requires, he may grant to one or several, determinate priests the faculty to administer this sacrament.

For a serious reason, as sometimes is present because of the large number of those to be confirmed, the bishop and also a priest who, in virtue of the law or a particular concession by competent authority, has the faculty to confirm, may in individual cases associate priests with himself so that they may administer the sacrament.

It is preferable that the priests who are so invited:
    a. either have a particular function or office in the diocese, being, namely, either vicars general, episcopal vicars, or district or regional vicars;
    b. or be the pastors of the places where confirmation is conferred, pastors of the places where the candidates belong, or priests who have had a special part in the catechetical preparation of the candidates.

III. CELEBRATION OF THE SACRAMENT

9. The sacrament of confirmation is conferred through the anointing with chrism on the forehead, which is done by the laying on of the hand, and through the words: BE SEALED WITH THE GIFT OF THE HOLY SPIRIT.

The laying of hands on the candidates with the prayer, *All-powerful God*, does not pertain to the valid giving of the sacrament. But it is still to be regarded as very important: it contributes to the complete perfection of the rite and to a more thorough understanding of the sacrament.

The priests who may at times be associated with the principal minister in conferring the sacrament join him in the laying of hands on all the candidates, but say nothing.

The whole rite presents a twofold symbolism. The laying of hands on the candidates by the bishop and the concelebrating priests represents the biblical gesture by which the gift of the Holy Spirit is invoked and in a manner well suited to the understanding of the Christian people. The anointing with chrism and the accompanying words express clearly the effect of the giving of the Holy Spirit. Signed with the perfumed oil, the baptized receive the indelible character, the seal of the Lord, together with the gift of the Spirit that conforms them more closely to Christ and gives them the grace of spreading "the sweet odor of Christ."

10. The chrism is consecrated by the bishop in the Mass that is celebrated as a rule on Holy Thursday for this purpose.

11. Adult catechumens and children who are baptized at an age when they are old enough for catechesis should ordinarily be admit-

ted to confirmation and the eucharist at the same time as they receive baptism. If this is impossible, they should receive confirmation at another community celebration (see no. 4). Similarly, adults who were baptized in infancy should, after suitable preparation, receive confirmation and the eucharist at a community celebration.

With regard to children, in the Latin Church the administration of confirmation is generally delayed until about the seventh year. For pastoral reasons, however, especially to implant deeply in the lives of the faithful complete obedience to Christ the Lord and a firm witnessing to him, the conferences of bishops may set an age that seems more suitable. This means that the sacrament is given, after the formation proper to it, when the recipients are more mature.

In this case every necessary precaution is to be taken to ensure that in the event of danger of death or serious problems of another kind children receive confirmation in good time, so that they are not left without the benefit of this sacrament.

12. Persons who are to receive confirmation must have already received baptism. Moreover, those possessing the use of reason must be in the state of grace, properly instructed, and capable of renewing the baptismal promises.

The conference of bishops has responsibility for determining more precisely the catechetical resources for the preparation of candidates for confirmation, especially children.

In the case of adults, those principles are to be followed, with the required adaptations, that apply in the individual dioceses to admitting catechumens to baptism and eucharist. Measures are to be taken especially for catechesis preceding confirmation and for the association of the candidates with the Christian community and with individual Christians. Such association is to be of a kind that is effective and sufficient as a practical help for the candidates to achieve formation toward both bearing witness by Christian living and carrying on the apostolate. It should also assist the candidates to have a genuine desire to share in the eucharist (see *Rite of Christian Initiation of Adults*, Introduction no. 19).

Sometimes the preparation of baptized adults for confirmation coincides with preparation for marriage. In such cases, if it is foreseen that the conditions for a fruitful reception of confirmation cannot be satisfied, the local Ordinary will judge whether it is better to defer confirmation until after the marriage.

If one who has the use of reason is confirmed in danger of death, there should, as far as possible, be some spiritual preparation beforehand, suited to the individual situation.

13. Confirmation takes place as a rule within Mass in order that the fundamental connection of this sacrament with all of Christian initiation may stand out in clearer light. Christian initiation reaches its culmination in the communion of the body and blood of Christ. The newly confirmed therefore participate in the eucharist, which completes their Christian initiation.

If the candidates for confirmation are children who have not received the eucharist and are not being admitted to first communion at this liturgical celebration or if there are other special circumstances, confirmation should be celebrated outside Mass. When this occurs, there is first to be a celebration of the word of God.

When confirmation is given during Mass, it is fitting that the minister of confirmation celebrate the Mass or, better, concelebrate it, especially with those priests who may be joining him in administering the sacrament.

If the Mass is celebrated by someone else, it is proper that the bishop preside over the liturgy of the word, doing all that the celebrant normally does, and that he give the blessing at the end of Mass.

Great emphasis should be placed on the celebration of the word of God that introduces the rite of confirmation. It is from the hearing of the word of God that the many-sided work of the Holy Spirit flows out upon the Church and upon each one of the baptized and confirmed. Through this hearing of his word God's will is made known in the life of Christians.

Great importance is likewise to be attached to the saying of the Lord's Prayer. Those to be confirmed will recite it together with the congregation — either during Mass before communion or outside Mass before the blessing — because it is the Spirit who prays in us and in the Spirit the Christian says: "Abba, Father."

14. The names of those confirmed, as well as the names of the minister, parents, and sponsors, and a notation of the place and date of the confirmation conferred, are to be entered into the registry of confirmations of the diocesan curia, or, where the conference of bishops or the diocesan bishop has so ordered, in a book to be kept in the parish archives. The pastor must inform the pastor of the recipient's place of baptism that confirmation has been conferred, so that this may be recorded in the baptismal register, according to the requirements of the law.

15. If the pastor of the place was not present, the minister should promptly inform him of the confirmation, either personally or through a representative.

IV. ADAPTATIONS PERMITTED IN THE RITE OF CONFIRMATION

16. By virtue of the Constitution on the Liturgy (art. 63 b), conferences of bishops have the right to prepare in particular rituals a section bearing the same title as the present title IV on confirmation in the Roman Pontifical. This is to be adapted to the needs of the individual parts of the world and it is to be used once the *acta* of the conference have been reviewed by the Apostolic See.[1]

---

[1] See *Rite of Baptism for Children,* General Introduction to Christian Initiation nos. 30-33.

17. The conference of bishops will consider whether, in view of local circumstances and the culture and traditions of the people, it is opportune:

    a. to make suitable adaptations of the formularies for the renewal of baptismal promises and professions, either following the text in the rite of baptism or accommodating these formularies so that they are more in accord with the circumstances of the candidates for confirmation;

    b. to introduce a different manner for the minister to give the sign of peace after the anointing, either to each individual or to all the newly confirmed together.

18. The minister of confirmation may introduce some explanations into the rite in individual cases in view of the capacity of the candidates for confirmation. He may also make appropriate accommodations in the existing texts, for example, by expressing these in a kind of dialogue, especially with children.

When confirmation is given by a minister who is not a bishop, whether by concession of the general law or by special indult of the Apostolic See, it is fitting for him to mention in the homily that the bishop is the original minister of the sacrament and to explain the reason why priests receive the faculty to confirm from the law or by an indult of the Apostolic See.

V. PREPARATIONS

19. The following should be prepared for the administration of confirmation:

    a. when confirmation is given within Mass, the vestments prescribed for the celebration of Mass both for the bishop and for any assisting priests who concelebrate with him. If the Mass is celebrated by someone else, the minister of confirmation as well as any priests joining him in administering the sacrament should take part in the Mass wearing the vestments prescribed for administering confirmation: alb, stole, and, for the minister, the cope; these also are the vestments worn when confirmation is given outside Mass;

    b. chairs for the bishop and the priests assisting him;

    c. vessel (or vessels) for the chrism;

    d. Roman Pontifical or Roman Ritual;

    e. when confirmation is given within Mass, the requisites for celebration of Mass and for communion under both kinds, if it is to be given;

    f. the requisites for the washing of hands after the anointing of those to be confirmed.

RITE OF CONFIRMATION WITHIN MASS

This Mass is celebrated, with red or white vestments, when confirmation is conferred within Mass or immediately before or after Mass.

It may be used on any day except the Sundays of Advent, Lent, and Easter, solemnities, Ash Wednesday, and Holy Week.

INTRODUCTORY RITES

Acts of prayer and penitence prepare us to meet Christ as he comes in Word and Sacrament. We gather as a worshiping community to celebrate our unity with him and with one another in faith.

Options are indicated by A, B, C, D in the margin. Hymns, antiphons, and other sung texts as selected from numbers given on pages 59-64.

ENTRANCE SONG **STAND**

Joined together as Christ's people, we open the celebration by raising our voices in praise of God who is present among us. This song should deepen our unity as it introduces the Mass we celebrate today.

If there is no singing, one of the following antiphons is recited.

ENTRANCE ANTIPHON Ezekiel 36:25-26

A I will pour clean water on you and I will give you a new heart, a new spirit within you, says the Lord.

or: Cf. Romans 5:5; 8:11

B The love of God has been poured into our hearts by his Spirit living in us.

After the entrance song, all make the sign of the cross:

Priest: In the name of the Father, and of the Son, and of the Holy Spirit.
People: Amen.

GREETING

The priest welcomes us in the name of the Lord. We show our union with God, our neighbor, and the priest by a united response to his greeting.

A Priest: The grace of our Lord Jesus Christ and the love of God and the fellowship of the Holy Spirit be with you all.
People: And also with you.

B Priest: The grace and peace of God our Father and the Lord Jesus Christ be with you.
People: Blessed be God, the Father of our Lord Jesus Christ.
or: And also with you.

C Priest: The Lord be with you. (Bishop: Peace be with you.)
People: And also with you.

RITE OF CONFIRMATION WITHIN MASS

PENITENTIAL RITE

After the introduction to the day's Mass, the priest invites the people to recall their sins and to repent of them in silence. He may use these or similar words:

A
As we prepare to celebrate the mystery of Christ's love,
let us acknowledge our failures
and ask the Lord for pardon and strength.

B
Coming together as God's family,
with confidence let us ask the Father's forgiveness,
for he is full of gentleness and compassion.

C
My brothers and sisters,
to prepare ourselves to celebrate the sacred mysteries,
let us call to mind our sins.

Then one of the following forms is used.

Priest and people:

A
> I confess to almighty God,
> and to you, my brothers and sisters,
> that I have sinned through my own fault
>
> *They strike their breast:*
>
> in my thoughts and in my words,
> in what I have done,
> and in what I have failed to do;
> and I ask blessed Mary, ever virgin,
> all the angels and saints,
> and you, my brothers and sisters,
> to pray for me to the Lord our God.

B
Priest: Lord, we have sinned against you:
Lord, have mercy.
People: Lord, have mercy.
Priest: Lord, show us your mercy and love.
People: And grant us your salvation.

C
Priest or other minister: *Invocation.*
Lord, have mercy.
People: Lord, have mercy.

Priest or other minister: *Invocation.*
Christ, have mercy.
People: Christ, have mercy.

Priest or other minister: *Invocation.*
Lord, have mercy.
People: Lord, have mercy.

At the end of any of the forms of the penitential rite:

Priest: May almighty God have mercy on us,
forgive us our sins,
and bring us to everlasting life.   People: Amen.

RITE OF CONFIRMATION WITHIN MASS

KYRIE

Unless included in the penitential rite, the Kyrie is sung or said by all, with alternating parts for the choir or cantor and for the people:

℣. Lord, have mercy.
℟. Lord, have mercy.
℣. Christ, have mercy.
℟. Christ, have mercy.
℣. Lord, have mercy.
℟. Lord, have mercy.

or:

℣. Kýrie, eleison.
℟. Kýrie, eleison.
℣. Christe, eleison.
℟. Christe, eleison.
℣. Kýrie, eleison.
℟. Kýrie, eleison.

1. LORD, HAVE MERCY
Joseph Roff
Org. Acc. 315

Lord, have mercy. Lord, have mercy.
Christ, have mercy. Christ, have mercy.
Lord, have mercy. Lord, have mercy.

GLORIA

As the Church assembled in the Spirit, we praise and pray to the Father and the Lamb.

When the Gloria is sung or said, the priest or the cantors or everyone together may begin it:

Glory to God in the highest,
and peace to his people on earth.
Lord God, heavenly King,
almighty God and Father,
we worship you, we give you thanks,
we praise you for your glory.
Lord Jesus Christ, only Son of the Father,
Lord God, Lamb of God,
you take away the sin of the world:
have mercy on us;
you are seated at the right hand of the Father:
receive our prayer.
For you alone are the Holy One,
you alone are the Lord,
you alone are the Most High,
Jesus Christ,
with the Holy Spirit,
in the glory of God the Father. Amen.

RITE OF CONFIRMATION WITHIN MASS

2. GLORY TO GOD IN THE HIGHEST

Joseph Roff
Org. Acc. 316

OPENING PRAYER

The priest invites us to pray silently for a moment and then, in our name, expresses the theme of the day's celebration and petitions God the Father through the mediation of Christ in the Holy Spirit.

Priest: Let us pray.

(Prayer in silence)

A God of power and mercy,
send your Holy Spirit to live in our hearts
and make us temples of his glory.

A
We ask you this through our Lord Jesus Christ, your Son,
who lives and reigns with you and the Holy Spirit,
one God, for ever and ever. **People:** Amen.

B
Lord,
fulfill your promise.
Send your Holy Spirit to make us witnesses before the world
to the Good News proclaimed by Jesus Christ, our Lord,
who lives and reigns with you and the Holy Spirit,
one God, for ever and ever. **People:** Amen.

C
Lord,
send us your Holy Spirit
to help us walk in unity of faith
and grow in the strength of his love
to the full stature of Christ,
who lives and reigns with you and the Holy Spirit,
one God, for ever and ever. **People:** Amen.

D
Lord,
fulfill the promise given by your Son
and send the Holy Spirit
to enlighten our minds
and lead us to all truth.
Grant this through our Lord Jesus Christ, your Son,
who lives and reigns with you and the Holy Spirit,
one God, for ever and ever. **People:** Amen.

LITURGY OF THE WORD

The proclamation of God's Word is always centered on Christ, present through his Word. Old Testament writings prepare for him; New Testament books speak of him directly. All of Scripture calls us to believe once more and to follow. After the reading we reflect upon God's words and respond to them.

SIT

20. The liturgy of the word is celebrated in the ordinary way. The readings may be taken from the Mass of the day or from the texts for confirmation as given here or as found on pages 48–58.

READING I   Ezek. 36:24-28

A reading from the book of the prophet Ezekiel

I will place a new Spirit in your midst

The Lord God said: I will take you away from among the nations, gather you from all the foreign lands, and bring you back to your own land. I will sprinkle clean water upon you to cleanse you from all your impurities, and from all your idols I will cleanse you. I will give you a new heart and place a new spirit within you, taking from your bodies your stony hearts and giving you natural hearts. I will put my spirit within you and make you live by my statutes, careful to observe my decrees. You shall live in the land I gave your fathers; you shall be my people and I will be your God.

> This is the Word of the Lord.

People: Thanks be to God.

RESPONSORIAL PSALM   Ps. 104:1, 24, 27-28, 30-31, 33-34

3. LORD, SEND OUT YOUR SPIRIT

Org. Acc. 363

Lord, send out your Spirit, and renew the face of the earth.

All repeat refrain; also after each verse.

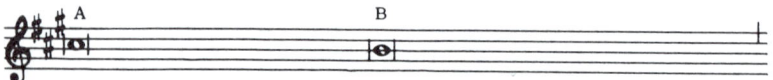

1. O Lord, my God,   you are great indeed!
2. When you give it to them,   they gather it;
3. and you renew the   face of the earth.
4. I will sing praise to my   God while I live.

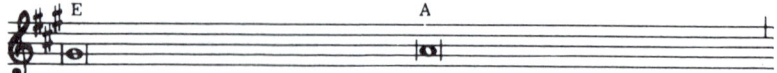

1. How manifold are your works, O Lord! In wisdom you have wrought them all--
2. When you open   your hand,
3. May the glory of the   Lord endure forever;
4. Pleasing to him   be my theme;

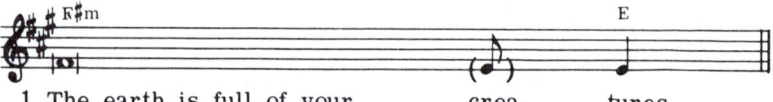

1. The earth is full of your   crea-   tures.
2. they are filled with good   things.
3. may the Lord be glad in his   works!
4. I will be glad in the   Lord.

READING II   Acts 8:1, 4, 14-17

A reading from the Acts of the Apostles

They laid hands on them, and they received the Holy Spirit

A certain day saw the beginning of a great persecution of the church in Jerusalem. All except the apostles scattered throughout the countryside of Judea and Samaria.

RITE OF CONFIRMATION WITHIN MASS

The members of the church who had been dispersed went about preaching the word.

When the apostles in Jerusalem heard that Samaria had accepted the word of God, they sent Peter and John to them. The two went down to these people and prayed that they might receive the Holy Spirit. It had not as yet come down upon any of them since they had been baptized in the name of the Lord Jesus. The pair upon arriving imposed hands on them and they received the Holy Spirit.

                                                          This is the Word of the Lord.

People: Thanks be to God.

ALLELUIA   **STAND**

Jesus will speak to us in the gospel. We rise now out of respect and prepare for his message with the alleluia.

4. ALLELUIA, COME, HOLY SPIRIT

℣. Al-le-lu-ia. ℟. Al-le-lu-ia.

℣. Come, Holy Spirit, fill the hearts of your faithful; and kindle in them the fire of your love.

℟. Al-le-lu-ia.

Before proclaiming the gospel, the priest says inaudibly: Almighty God, cleanse my heart and my lips that I may worthily proclaim your gospel.

Priest: The Lord be with you.
People: And also with you.

GOSPEL   John 14:23-26

✠ A reading from the holy gospel according to John

People: Glory to you, Lord.

The Holy Spirit will teach you everything

Jesus said to his disciples:
"Anyone who loves me
will be true to my word,
and my Father will love him;

we will come to him
and make our dwelling place with him.
He who does not love me does not keep my words.
Yet the word you hear is not mine;
it comes from the Father who sent me.
This much have I told you while I was still with you;
the Paraclete, the Holy Spirit
whom the Father will send in my name,
will instruct you in everything,
and remind you of all that I told you.''

This is the gospel of the Lord.

People: Praise to you, Lord Jesus Christ.

Then the priest kisses the book, saying inaudibly: May the words of the gospel wipe away our sins.

Presentation of the Candidates

21. After the gospel the bishop and the priests who assist him are seated. The pastor or another priest, deacon, or catechist presents the candidates for confirmation according to the custom of the region. If possible, each candidate is called by name and comes individually to the sanctuary. If the candidates are children, they are accompanied by one of their sponsors or parents and both stand before the celebrant.

If there are many candidates, they are not called by name, but take a suitable place before the bishop.

Homily

22. The bishop then gives a brief homily. He should explain the readings and lead the candidates, their sponsors and parents, and the whole assembly to a deeper understanding of the mystery of confirmation.

He may use these or similar words:

At Pentecost the apostles received the Holy Spirit as the Lord had promised. They also received the power of giving the Holy Spirit and so completing the work of baptism. This we read in the Acts of the Apostles. When Saint Paul placed his hands on those who had been baptized, the Holy Spirit came upon them, and they began to speak in other languages and prophetic words.

Bishops are successors of the apostles and have this power of giving the Holy Spirit to the baptized, either personally or through the priests they appoint.

In our day the coming of the Holy Spirit is not usually marked by the gift of tongues, but we know his coming by faith. He fills our hearts with the love of God, brings us together in one faith but in different vocations, and works within us to make the Church one and holy.

The gift of the Holy Spirit which you are to receive will be a spiritual sign and seal to make you more Christ-like and more perfect members of his Church. At his baptism by John, Christ was anointed by the Spirit and sent out on his public ministry to set the world on fire.

You have already been baptized into Christ and now you will receive the power of his Spirit and the sign of the cross on your forehead. You must be witnesses before all the world to his suffering, death, and resurrection; your way of life should reflect the goodness of Christ. Christ gives varied gifts to his Church, and the Spirit distributes them among the members of Christ's body to build up the holy people of God in unity and love.

Be active members of the Church, alive in Jesus Christ. Under the guidance of the Holy Spirit give your lives completely in the service of all, as did Christ, who came not to be served but to serve.

Before you receive the Spirit, renew the profession of faith you made in baptism or your parents and godparents made for you in union with the whole Church.

RENEWAL OF BAPTISMAL PROMISES

23. After the homily the candidates stand and the bishop questions them. They respond together.

Bishop: Do you reject Satan and all his works and all his empty promises?

Candidates: I do.

Bishop: Do you believe in God the Father almighty, creator of heaven and earth?

Candidates: I do.

Bishop: Do you believe in Jesus Christ, his only Son, our Lord, who was born of the Virgin Mary, was crucified, died, and was buried, rose from the dead, and is now seated at the right hand of the Father?

Candidates: I do.

Bishop: Do you believe in the Holy Spirit, the Lord, the giver of life, who came upon the apostles at Pentecost and today is given to you sacramentally in confirmation?

Candidates: I do.

Bishop: Do you believe in the holy catholic Church, the communion of saints, the forgiveness of sins, the resurrection of the body, and life everlasting?

Candidates: I do.

The bishop gives his assent to their profession of faith and proclaims the faith of the Church:

> This is our faith. This is the faith of the Church.
> We are proud to profess it in Christ Jesus our Lord.

The congregation responds:

> Amen.

For This is our faith, some other formula may be substituted, or the community may express its faith in a suitable song (see pages 59–64).

THE LAYING ON OF HANDS

The laying of hands on the candidates by the bishop and concelebrating priests expresses the biblical gesture by which the gift of the Holy Spirit is invoked.

24. While the priests who assist the bishop stand near him, he stands facing the people, and with hands joined, sings or says:

My dear friends:

in baptism God our Father gave the new birth of eternal life
to his chosen sons and daughters.
Let us pray to our Father
that he will pour out the Holy Spirit
to strengthen his sons and daughters with his gifts
and anoint them to be more like Christ the Son of God.

All pray in silence for a short time.

25. The bishop and the priests who assist him extend their hands over all the candidates. The bishop alone sings or says:

All-powerful God, Father of our Lord Jesus Christ,
by water and the Holy Spirit
you freed your sons and daughters from sin
and gave them new life.
Send your Holy Spirit upon them
to be their Helper and Guide.
Give them the spirit of wisdom and understanding,
the spirit of right judgment and courage,
the spirit of knowledge and reverence.
Fill them with the spirit of wonder and awe in your presence.
We ask this through Christ our Lord.

People: Amen.

ANOINTING

Through the anointing with chrism (perfumed oil) the baptized person receives the indelible character, the seal of the Lord, together with the gift of the Spirit which conforms him/her more closely to Christ and gives the grace of spreading the Lord's presence among all people.

26. The deacon brings the chrism to the bishop. Each candidate goes to the bishop, or the bishop may go to the individual candidates. The one who presented the candidate places his/her right hand on the latter's shoulder and gives the candidate's name to the bishop; the candidate, however, may give his/her own name.

RITE OF CONFIRMATION WITHIN MASS

27. The bishop dips his right thumb in the chrism and makes the sign of the cross on the forehead of the one to be confirmed as he says:

N., be sealed with the Gift of the Holy Spirit.

The newly-confirmed responds: Amen.

The bishop says: Peace be with you.

The newly-confirmed responds: And also with you.

28. If priests assist the bishop in conferring the sacrament, all the vessels of chrism are brought to the bishop by the deacon or by other ministers. The bishop gives a vessel of chrism to each of the priests.

The candidates go to the bishop or to the priests, or the bishop and priests may go to the candidates. The anointing is done as described above.

29. During the anointing a suitable song may be sung (see pages 59–64). After the anointing the bishop and the priests wash their hands.

GENERAL INTERCESSIONS (PRAYER OF THE FAITHFUL)

As a priestly people we unite with one another to pray for today's needs in the Church and the world.

30. The celebrant introduces the Prayer of the Faithful with the following form or a similar one approved by the competent authority.

Bishop:

My dear friends, let us be one in prayer to God our Father as we are one in the faith, hope, and love his Spirit gives.

Deacon or minister:

For these sons and daughters of God, confirmed by the gift of the Spirit, that they give witness to Christ by lives built on faith and love, let us pray to the Lord:

People: Lord, hear our prayer.

Deacon or minister:

For the newly confirmed, who have received the fullness of God's Spirit, that standing at the altar of the Lord they may share the banquet of Christ's sacrifice, calling God their Father in the midst of the Church, let us pray to the Lord:

People: Lord, hear our prayer.

Deacon or minister:

For the parents and godparents who led them in faith, that by word and example they may always encourage them to follow the ways of Jesus Christ, let us pray to the Lord:

People: Lord, hear our prayer.

Deacon or minister:
For the holy Church of God, in union with N. our pope, N. our bishop, and all the bishops, that God, who gathers us together by the Holy Spirit, may help us grow in unity of faith and love until his Son returns in glory, let us pray to the Lord:

People: Lord, hear our prayer.

Deacon or minister:
For all men and women, of every race and nation, that they may acknowledge the one God as Father, and in the bond of common fellowship seek his kingdom, which is peace and joy in the Holy Spirit, let us pray to the Lord:

People: Lord, hear our prayer.

Bishop: God our Father,
you sent the Holy Spirit upon the apostles,
and through them and their successors
you give the Spirit to your people.
May his work begun at Pentecost
continue to grow in the hearts of all who believe.
We ask this through Christ our Lord.

People: Amen.

LITURGY OF THE EUCHARIST

Made ready by reflection on God's Word, we enter now into the Eucharistic sacrifice itself, the Supper of the Lord. We celebrate the memorial which the Lord instituted at his Last Supper. We are God's new people, the redeemed brothers and sisters of Christ, gathered by him around his table. We are here to bless God and to receive the gift of Jesus' Body and Blood so that our faith and life may be transformed.

PREPARATION OF THE GIFTS **SIT**

31. Some of the newly confirmed may join those who bring the gifts to the altar.
32. Adults who are confirmed, their sponsors, parents, wives and husbands, and catechists may receive communion under both kinds.

While the gifts are placed on the altar, the offertory song is sung, see pages 59-64. Before placing the bread on the altar, the priest says inaudibly.

> Blessed are you, Lord, God of all creation.
> Through your goodness we have this bread to offer,
> which earth has given and human hands have made.
> It will become for us the bread of life.

If there is no singing, the priest may say this prayer aloud, and the people may respond:

> Blessed be God for ever.

When he pours wine and a little water into the chalice, the deacon (or the priest) says inaudibly:

> By the mystery of this water and wine
> may we come to share in the divinity of Christ,
> who humbled himself to share in our humanity.

Before placing the chalice on the altar, the priest says inaudibly:

> Blessed are you, Lord, God of all creation.
> Through your goodness we have this wine to offer,
> fruit of the vine and work of human hands.
> It will become our spiritual drink.

If there is no singing, the priest may say this prayer aloud, and the people may respond:

> Blessed be God for ever.

The priest says inaudibly:

> Lord God, we ask you to receive us
> and be pleased with the sacrifice we offer you
> with humble and contrite hearts.

Then he washes his hands, saying inaudibly:

> Lord, wash away my iniquity;
> cleanse me from my sin.

INVITATION TO PRAYER

Priest: Pray, brethren, that our sacrifice
may be acceptable to God, the almighty Father.

People: May the Lord accept the sacrifice at your hands
for the praise and glory of his name,
for our good, and the good of all his Church.

PRAYER OVER THE GIFTS   **STAND**

The priest, speaking in our name, asks the Father to bless and accept these gifts.

A
Lord,
we celebrate the memorial of our redemption
by which your Son won for us the gift of the Holy Spirit.
Accept our offerings,
and send us your Spirit
to make us more like Christ
in bearing witness to the world.
We ask this through Christ our Lord. **People:** Amen.

B Lord,
you have signed our brothers and sisters
with the cross of your Son
and anointed them with the oil of salvation.
As they offer themselves with Christ,
continue to fill their hearts with your Spirit.
We ask this through Christ our Lord. People: Amen.

C Lord,
accept the offering of your family
and help those who receive the gift of your Spirit
to keep him in their hearts
and come to the reward of eternal life.
We ask this through Christ our Lord. People: Amen.

THE EUCHARISTIC PRAYER

We begin the Eucharistic service of praise and thanksgiving, the center of the entire celebration, the central prayer of worship. At the priest's invitation we lift our hearts to God and unite with him in the words he addresses to the Father through Jesus Christ. Together we join Christ in his sacrifice, celebrating his memorial in the holy meal and acknowledging with him the wonderful works of God in our lives.

INTRODUCTORY DIALOGUE

Priest: The Lord be with you.
People: And also with you.

Priest: Lift up your hearts.
People: We lift them up to the Lord.

Priest: Let us give thanks to the Lord our God.
People: It is right to give him thanks and priase.

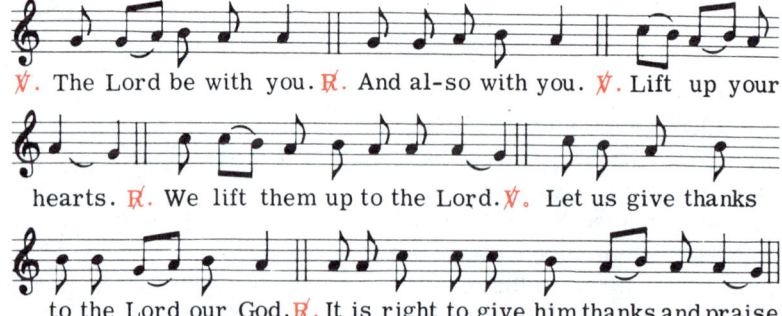

℣. The Lord be with you. ℟. And al-so with you. ℣. Lift up your hearts. ℟. We lift them up to the Lord. ℣. Let us give thanks to the Lord our God. ℟. It is right to give him thanks and praise.

PREFACE OF THE HOLY SPIRIT

Father, all-powerful and ever-living God,
we do well always and everywhere to give you thanks
through Jesus Christ our Lord.

He ascended above all the heavens,
and from his throne at your right hand
poured into the hearts of your adopted children
the Holy Spirit of your promise.

With steadfast love
we sing your unending praise;
we join with the hosts of heaven
in their triumphant song:

SANCTUS

Priest and people: Holy, holy, holy Lord, God of power and might,
heaven and earth are full of your glory.
Hosanna in the highest.
Blessed is he who comes in the name of the Lord.
Hosanna in the highest.

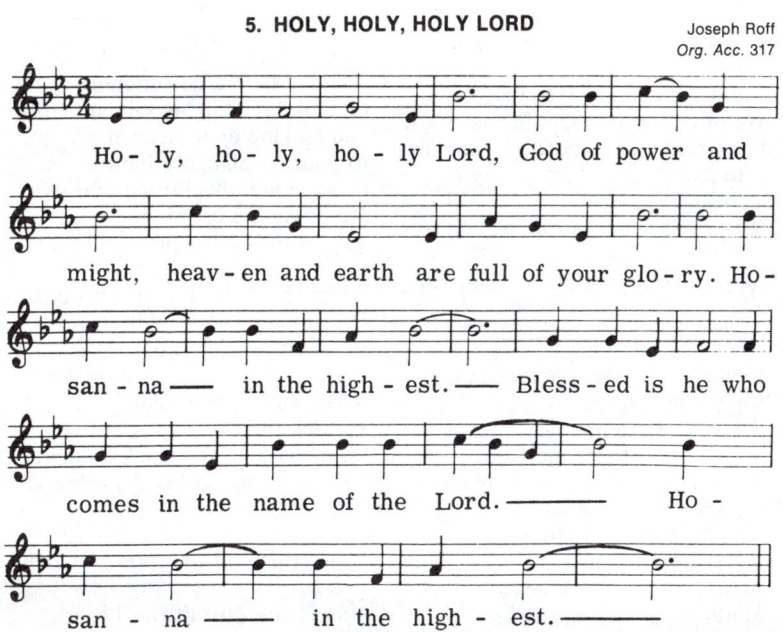

5. HOLY, HOLY, HOLY LORD
Joseph Roff
Org. Acc. 317

Ho-ly, ho-ly, ho-ly Lord, God of power and might, heav-en and earth are full of your glo-ry. Ho-san-na in the high-est. Bless-ed is he who comes in the name of the Lord. Ho-san-na in the high-est.

The people kneel after the Sanctus **is sung or said.** **KNEEL**

EUCHARISTIC PRAYER I (THE ROMAN CANON)

Praise to the Father

We come to you, Father,
with praise and thanksgiving,
through Jesus Christ your Son.
Through him we ask you to accept
   and bless ✠
these gifts we offer you in sacrifice.

Intercessions: for the Church

We offer them for your holy catholic
   Church,
watch over it, Lord, and guide it;
grant it peace and unity throughout
   the world.
We offer them for N. our Pope,
for N. our bishop,
and for all who hold and teach the
   catholic faith
that comes to us from the apostles.

Remember, Lord, your people,
especially those for whom we now
   pray, N. and N.
Remember all of us gathered here
   before you.
You know how firmly we believe in
   you
and dedicate ourselves to you.
We offer you this sacrifice of praise
for ourselves and those who are dear
   to us.

We pray to you, our living and true
   God,
for our well-being and redemption.

In communion with the Saints

In union with the whole Church
we honor Mary,
the ever-virgin mother of Jesus
   Christ our Lord and God.
We honor Joseph, her husband,
the apostles and martyrs
Peter and Paul, Andrew,
(James, John, Thomas,
James, Philip, Bartholomew,
Matthew, Simon and Jude;
we honor Linus, Cletus, Clement,
   Sixtus,
Cornelius, Cyprian, Lawrence,
Chrysogonus, John and Paul,
Cosmas and Damian)
and all the saints.
May their merits and prayers
gain us your constant help and pro-
   tection.
(Through Christ our Lord. Amen.)

Father, accept this offering
from your whole family,
and from those reborn in baptism
and confirmed by the coming of
   the Holy Spirit.
Protect them with your love and
   keep them close to you.
(Through Christ our Lord. Amen.)

Bless and approve our offering;
make it acceptable to you,
an offering in spirit and in truth.
Let it become for us
the body and blood of Jesus Christ,
your only Son, our Lord.

The Lord's Supper

The day before he suffered
he took bread in his sacred hands
and looking up to heaven,
to you, his almighty Father,
he gave you thanks and praise.
He broke the bread,
gave it to his disciples, and said:

Take this, all of you, and eat it:
this is my body which will be
   given up for you.

When supper was ended,
he took the cup.
Again he gave you thanks and praise,
gave the cup to his disciples, and
   said:

Take this, all of you, and drink
   from it:
this is the cup of my blood,
the blood of the new and everlasting covenant.

It will be shed for you and for all
so that sins may be forgiven.
Do this in memory of me.

Then he says:
Let us proclaim the mystery of faith:
Melody, page 30

A
Christ has died,
Christ is risen,
Christ will come again.

B
Dying you destroyed our death,
rising you restored our life.
Lord Jesus, come in glory.

C
When we eat this bread and drink this cup,
we proclaim your death, Lord Jesus,
until you come in glory.

D
Lord, by your cross and resurrection
you have set us free.
You are the Savior of the world.

The memorial prayer
Father, we celebrate the memory of Christ, your Son.
We, your people and your ministers, recall his passion,
his resurrection from the dead,
and his ascension into glory;
and from the many gifts you have given us
we offer to you, God of glory and majesty,
this holy and perfect sacrifice:
the bread of life
and the cup of eternal salvation.

Look with favor on these offerings
and accept them as once you accepted
the gifts of your servant Abel,
the sacrifice of Abraham, our father in faith,
and the bread and wine offered by your priest Melchisedech.

Almighty God,
we pray that your angel may take this sacrifice
to your altar in heaven.
Then, as we receive from this altar
the sacred body and blood of your Son,
let us be filled with every grace and blessing.
(Through Christ our Lord. Amen.)

For the dead
Remember, Lord, those who have died
and have gone before us marked with the sign of faith,
especially those for whom we now pray, N. and N.
May these, and all who sleep in Christ,
find in your presence
light, happiness, and peace.
(Through Christ our Lord. Amen.)

For ourselves, too, we ask
some share in the fellowship of your apostles and martyrs,
with John the Baptist, Stephen, Matthias, Barnabas,
(Ignatius, Alexander, Marcellinus, Peter,
Felicity, Perpetua, Agatha, Lucy,
Agnes, Cecilia, Anastasia)
and all the saints.
Though we are sinners,
we trust in your mercy and love.
Do not consider what we truly deserve,
but grant us your forgiveness.
Through Christ our Lord.
Through him you give us all these gifts.
You fill them with life and goodness.
you bless them and make them holy.

Concluding doxology
Through him,
with him,
in him,
in the unity of the Holy Spirit,
all glory and honor is yours,
almighty Father,
for ever and ever.

The people respond: Amen.
Sung Amen, page 35.
Turn to the Lord's Prayer, *page 35.*

PREFACE TO EUCHARISTIC PRAYER II

Father, it is our duty and our salvation,
always and everywhere
to give you thanks
through your beloved Son, Jesus Christ.
He is the Word through whom you made the universe,
the Savior you sent to redeem us.
By the power of the Holy Spirit
he took flesh and was born of the Virgin Mary.
For our sake he opened his arms on the cross;
he put an end to death
and revealed the resurrection.
In this he fulfilled your will
and won for you a holy people.
And so we join the angels and the saints in proclaiming your glory as we sing (say):

EUCHARISTIC PRAYER II

Lord, you are holy indeed,
the fountain of all holiness.
Let your Spirit come upon these gifts to make them holy,
so that they may become for us
the body ✠ and blood of our Lord, Jesus Christ.

The Lord's Supper

Before he was given up to death,
a death he freely accepted,
he took bread and gave you thanks.
He broke the bread,
gave it to his disciples and said:

Take this, all of you, and eat it:
this is my body which will be given up for you.

When supper was ended, he took the cup.
Again he gave you thanks and praise,
gave the cup to his disciples, and said:

Take this, all of you, and drink from it:
this is the cup of my blood,
the blood of the new and everlasting covenant.
It will be shed for you and for all
so that sins may be forgiven.

Do this in memory of me.

Priest: Let us proclaim the mystery of faith:

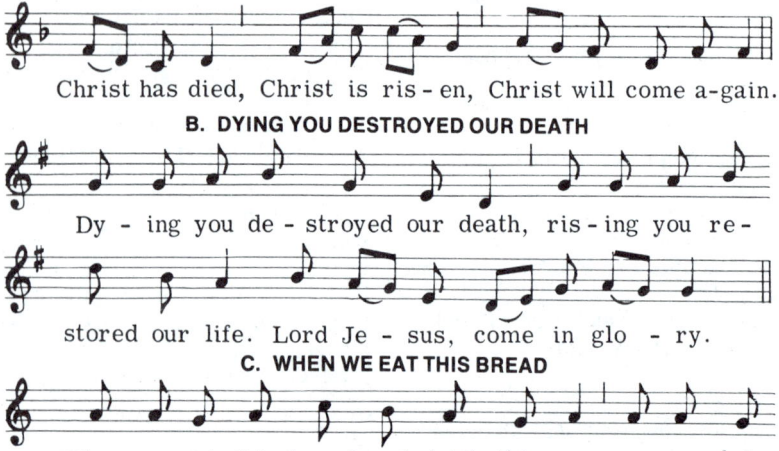

A. CHRIST HAS DIED
Christ has died, Christ is ris-en, Christ will come a-gain.

B. DYING YOU DESTROYED OUR DEATH
Dy-ing you de-stroyed our death, ris-ing you re-stored our life. Lord Je-sus, come in glo-ry.

C. WHEN WE EAT THIS BREAD
When we eat this bread and drink this cup, we pro-claim

RITE OF CONFIRMATION WITHIN MASS

your death, Lord Jesus, until you come in glory.

D. LORD, BY YOUR CROSS

Lord, by your cross and resurrection you have

set us free. You are the Savior of the world.

The memorial prayer
In memory of his death and resurrection,
we offer you, Father, this life-giving bread,
this saving cup,
We thank you for counting us worthy
to stand in your presence and serve you.

Invocations of the Holy Spirit
May all of us who share in the body and blood of Christ
be brought together in unity by the Holy Spirit.

Intercessions: for the Church
Lord, remember your Church throughout the world;
make us grow in love,
together with N. our Pope,
N. our bishop, and all the clergy.

For the dead
Remember our brothers and sisters
who have gone to their rest
in the hope of rising again;
bring them and all the departed
into the light of your presence.

In communion with the Saints
Have mercy on us all;
make us worthy to share eternal life
with Mary, the virgin mother of God,
with the apostles,
and with all the saints who have done your will throughout the ages.
May we praise you in union with them, and give you glory
through your Son, Jesus Christ.

Concluding doxology
Through him,
with him,
in him,
in the unity of the Holy Spirit,
all glory and honor is yours.
almighty Father,
for ever and ever

The people respond: Amen

Sung Amen, page 35.

Turn to the Lord's Prayer, *page 35.*

EUCHARISTIC PRAYER III

Praise to the Father
Father, you are holy indeed,
and all creation rightly gives you praise.
All life, all holiness comes from you
through your Son, Jesus Christ our Lord,
by the working of the Holy Spirit.
From age to age you gather a people to yourself,
so that from east to west
a perfect offering may be made
to the glory of your name.

RITE OF CONFIRMATION WITHIN MASS

Invocation of the Holy Spirit

D And so, Father, we bring you these gifts.
We ask you to make them holy by the power of your Spirit,
that they may become the body ✠ and blood
of your Son, our Lord Jesus Christ,
at whose command we celebrate this eucharist.

The Lord's Supper

On the night he was betrayed,
he took bread and gave you thanks and praise.
He broke the bread, gave it to his disciples, and said:

Take this, all of you, and eat it:
this is my body which will be given up for you.

When supper was ended, he took the cup.
Again he gave you thanks and praise,
gave the cup to his disciples, and said:

Take this, all of you, and drink from it:
this is the cup of my blood,
the blood of the new and everlasting covenant.
It will be shed for you and for all so that sins may be forgiven.

Do this in memory of me.

Priest: Let us proclaim the mystery of faith: *Melody, page 30.*

A
Christ has died,
Christ is risen,
Christ will come again.

B
Dying you destroyed our death,
rising you restored our life.
Lord Jesus, come in glory.

C
When we eat this bread and drink this cup,
we proclaim your death, Lord Jesus,
until you come in glory.

Lord, by your cross and resurrection you have set us free.
You are the Savior of the world.

The memorial prayer

Father, calling to mind the death your Son endured for our salvation,
his glorious resurrection and ascension into heaven,
and ready to greet him when he comes again,
we offer you in thanksgiving this holy and living sacrifice.
Look with favor on your Church's offering,
and see the Victim whose death has reconciled us to yourself.

Invocation of the Holy Spirit

Grant that we, who are nourished by his body and blood,
may be filled with his Holy Spirit,
and become one body, one spirit in Christ.

Intercessions: in communion with the Saints

May he make us an everlasting gift to you
and enable us to share in the inheritance of your saints,
with Mary, the virgin mother of God;
with the apostles, the martyrs,
(Saint N. — the patron saint or the saint of the day) and all your saints,
on whose constant intercession we rely for help.

For the Church

Lord, may this sacrifice, which has made our peace with you,
advance the peace and salvation of all the world.
Strengthen in faith and love your pilgrim Church on earth;
your servant, Pope N., our bishop N. and all the bishops,
with the clergy and the entire people your Son has gained for you.
Father, hear the prayers of the family you have gathered here before you.

In mercy and love unite all your children
wherever they may be.

For the dead

Welcome into your kingdom our departed brothers and sisters,
and all who have left this world in your friendship.
We hope to enjoy for ever the vision of your glory,
through Christ our Lord, from whom all good things come.

Concluding doxology

Through him,
with him,
in him,
in the unity of the Holy Spirit,
all glory and honor is yours,
almighty Father,
for ever and ever.

The people respond: Amen.

Sung Amen, page 35.

Turn to the Lord's Prayer, page 35.

PREFACE TO EUCHARISTIC PRAYER IV

Father in heaven, it is right that we should give you thanks and glory:
you are the one God, living and true.
Through all eternity you live in unapproachable light.
Source of life and goodness, you have created all things,
to fill your creatures with every blessing
and lead all men to the joyful vision of your light.
Countless hosts of angels stand before you to do your will;
they look upon your splendor
and praise you, night and day.
United with them, and in the name of every creature under heaven,
we too praise your glory as we sing (say):

EUCHARISTIC PRAYER IV

Praise to the Father

Father, we acknowledge your greatness:
all your actions show your wisdom and love.
You formed man in your own likeness
and set him over the whole world
to serve you, his creator,
and to rule over all creatures.
Even when he disobeyed you and lost your friendship
you did not abandon him to the power of death,
but helped all men to seek and find you.
Again and again you offered a covenant to man,
and through the prophets taught him to hope for salvation.
Father, you so loved the world
that in the fullness of time you sent your only Son to be our Savior.
He was conceived through the power of the Holy Spirit, and born of the Virgin Mary,
a man like us in all things but sin.
To the poor he proclaimed the good news of salvation,
to prisoners, freedom,
and to those in sorrow, joy.
In fulfillment of your will
he gave himself up to death;
but by rising from the dead,
he destroyed death and restored life.
And that we might live no longer for ourselves but for him,
he sent the Holy Spirit from you, Father,
as his first gift to those who believe,
to complete his work on earth
and bring us the fullness of grace.

Invocation of the Holy Spirit

Father, may this Holy Spirit sanctify these offerings.
Let them become the body ✠ and blood of Jesus Christ our Lord
as we celebrate the great mystery
which he left us as an everlasting covenant.

The Lord's Supper

He always loved those who were his own in the world.
When the time came for him to be glorified by you, his heavenly Father,
he showed the depth of his love.
While they were at supper,
he took bread, said the blessing, broke the bread
and gave it to his disciples, saying:

Take this, all of you, and eat it:
this is my body which will be given up for you.

In the same way, he took the cup, filled with wine.
He gave you thanks, and giving the cup to his disciples, said:

Take this, all of you, and drink from it:
this is the cup of my blood,
the blood of the new and everlasting covenant.
It will be shed for you and for all so that sins may be forgiven.

Do this in memory of me.

Priest: Let us proclaim the mystery of faith: *Melody, page 30.*

A Christ has died,
Christ is risen,
Christ will come again.

B Dying you destroyed our death,
rising you restored our life.
Lord Jesus, come in glory.

C When we eat this bread and drink this cup,
we proclaim your death, Lord Jesus, until you come in glory.

D Lord, by your cross and resurrection you have set us free.
You are the Savior of the world.

The memorial prayer

Father, we now celebrate this memorial of our redemption.
We recall Christ's death, his descent among the dead,
his resurrection, and his ascension to your right hand;
and, looking forward to his coming in glory, we offer you his body and blood,
the acceptable sacrifice which brings salvation to the whole world.
Lord, look upon this sacrifice which you have given to your Church;
and by your Holy Spirit, gather all who share this one bread and one cup
into the one body of Christ, a living sacrifice of praise.

Intercessions: for the Church

Lord, remember those for whom we offer this sacrifice,
especially N. our Pope,
N. our bishop, and bishops and clergy everywhere.
Remember those who take part in this offering,
those here present and all your people,
and all who seek you with a sincere heart.

For the dead

Remember those who have died in the peace of Christ
and all the dead whose faith is known to you alone.

In communion with the Saints

Father, in your mercy grant also to us, your children,
to enter into our heavenly inheritance
in the company of the Virgin Mary, the Mother of God,
and your apostles and saints.
Then, in your kingdom, freed from the corruption of sin and death,
we shall sing your glory with every creature through Christ our Lord,

RITE OF CONFIRMATION WITHIN MASS

through whom you give us everything that is good.

Concluding doxology

Through him,
with him,
in him,
in the unity of the Holy Spirit,
all glory and honor is yours,
almighty Father,
for ever and ever.

The people respond: Amen.

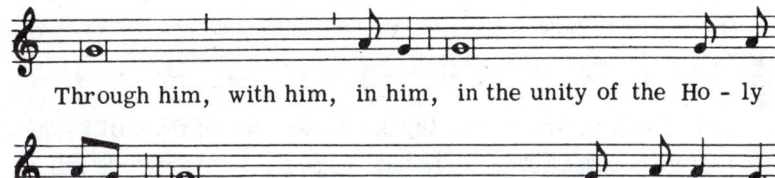

Through him, with him, in him, in the unity of the Holy Spirit, all glory and honor is yours almighty Father, forever and ever. *All:* A-men.

6. EUCHARISTIC PRAYER: AMEN

Org. Acc. 285
(Danish)

A-men, A-men, A-men.

Alternate melody.

Org. Acc. 286

A-men. A-men. A-men.

COMMUNION RITE

To prepare for the paschal meal, to welcome the Lord, we pray for forgiveness and exchange a sign of peace. Before eating Christ's Body and drinking his Blood, we must be one with him and with all our brothers and sisters in the Church.

LORD'S PRAYER **STAND**

Priest:

A Let us pray with confidence to the Father in the words our Savior gave us:

B Jesus taught us to call God our Father, and so we have the courage to say:

C Let us ask our Father to forgive our sins and to bring us to forgive those who sin against us.

D Let us pray for the coming of the kingdom as Jesus taught us.

RITE OF CONFIRMATION WITHIN MASS

Priest: Let us pray with confidence to the Father in the words our Savior gave us. **All:** Our Father, who art in heaven, hallowed be thy name; thy kingdom come; thy will be done on earth as it is in heaven. Give us this day our daily bread; and forgive us our trespasses as we forgive those who trespass against us; and lead us not into temptation, but deliver us from evil.

Priest: Deliver us, Lord, from every evil,
and grant us peace in our day.
In your mercy keep us free from sin
and protect us from all anxiety
as we wait in joyful hope
for the coming of our Savior, Jesus Christ.

People: For the kingdom, the power, and the glory are yours, now and for ever.

For the kingdom, the power and the glory are yours, now and for ever.

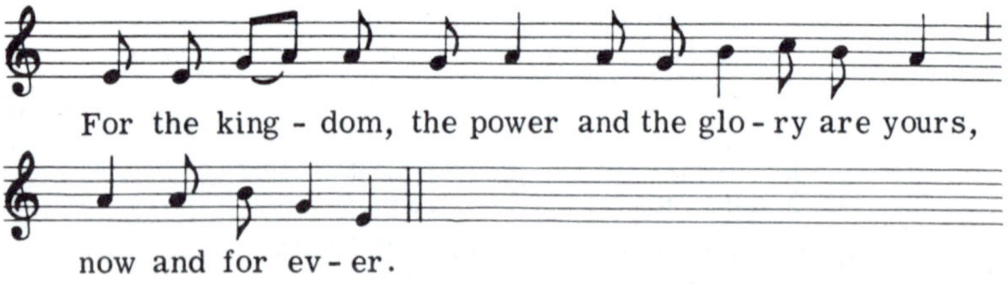

SIGN OF PEACE

The priest says the prayer for peace:

Lord Jesus Christ, you said to your apostles:
I leave you peace, my peace I give you.

Look not on our sins, but on the faith of your Church,
and grant us the peace and unity of your kingdom
where you live for ever and ever. All: Amen.

Priest: The peace of the Lord be with you always.
People: And also with you.

The peace of the Lord be with you al-ways. All: And al-so with you.

Then the deacon (or the priest) may add:
Let us offer each other the sign of peace.

BREAKING OF THE BREAD

The priest breaks the host over the paten and places a small piece in the chalice, saying inaudibly:

May this mingling of the body and blood of our Lord Jesus Christ bring eternal life to us who receive it.

Meanwhile the people sing or say:

Lamb of God, you take away the sins of the world:
 have mercy on us.

Lamb of God, you take away the sins of the world:
 have mercy on us.

Lamb of God, you take away the sins of the world:
 grant us peace.

7. LAMB OF GOD

Joseph Roff
Org. Acc. 318

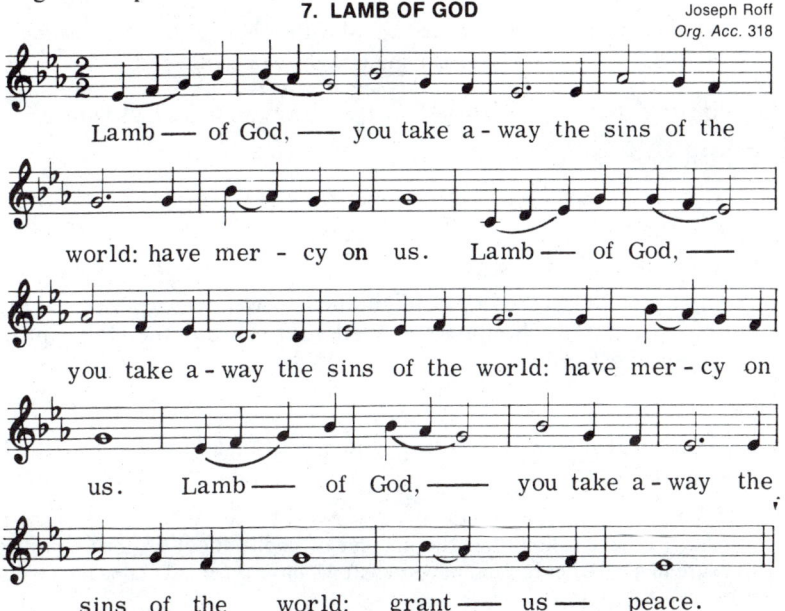

COMMUNION

We pray in silence and then voice words of humility and hope as our final preparation before meeting Christ in the Eucharist.

Before communion, the priest says inaudibly one of the following prayers:

A Lord Jesus Christ, Son of the living God,
by the will of the Father and the work of the Holy Spirit
your death brought life to the world.
By your holy body and blood
free me from all my sins and from every evil.
Keep me faithful to your teaching,
and never let me be parted from you.

or

B Lord Jesus Christ,
with faith in your love and mercy
I eat your body and drink your blood.
Let it not bring me condemnation,
but health in mind and body.

Priest: This is the Lamb of God
who takes away the sins of the world.
Happy are those who are called to his supper.

Priest and people (once only):
Lord, I am not worthy to receive you,
but only say the word and I shall be healed.

Before receiving communion, the priest says inaudibly: May the body of Christ bring me to everlasting life, **and** May the blood of Christ bring me to everlasting life. **He then gives communion to the people.**

Priest: The body of Christ.   **Communicant:** Amen.

COMMUNION SONG

After communion there may be a period of silence, or a song of praise may be sung. If there is no singing, one of the following antiphons is recited.

COMMUNION ANTIPHON   Cf. Hebrews 6:4

A All of you who have been enlightened, who have experienced the gift of heaven and who have received your share of the Holy Spirit, rejoice in the Lord.

or: Psalm 33:6, 9

B Look up at him with gladness and smile; taste and see the goodness of the Lord.

If the priest cleanses the vessels, he says the following prayer inaudibly:
What we have taken after the manner of bodily food, O Lord, may we treasure in a pure heart. And may the gift we have received in this life be our provision for eternity.

Prayer after Communion

Priest: Let us pray.

(Prayer in silence)

A
Lord,
help those you have anointed by your Spirit
and fed with the body and blood of your Son.
Support them through every trial
and by their works of love
build up the Church in holiness and joy.
Grant this through Christ our Lord. **People:** Amen.

B
Lord,
you give your Son as food
to those you anoint with your Spirit.
Help them to fulfill your law
by living in freedom as your children.
May they live in holiness
and be your witnesses to the world.
We ask this through Christ our Lord. **People:** Amen.

C
Lord,
we have shared the one bread of life.
Send the Spirit of your love
to keep us one in faith and peace.
We ask this through Christ our Lord. **People:** Amen.

Priest: The Lord be with you.
People: And also with you.

Blessing

33. In place of the usual blessing, the following blessing or prayer over the people is used.

The deacon or minister gives the invitation in these or similar words: Bow your heads and pray for God's blessing.

The bishop extends his hands over the people and sings or says:

A
God our Father
made you his children by water and the Holy Spirit:
may he bless you
and watch over you with his fatherly love.
People: Amen.

Jesus Christ the Son of God
promised that the Spirit of truth
would be with his Church for ever:
may he bless you and give you courage
in professing the true faith.
People: Amen.

A

> The Holy Spirit
> came down upon the disciples
> and set their hearts on fire with love:
> may he bless you,
> keep you one in faith and love
> and bring you to the joy of God's kingdom.

People: Amen.

The bishop adds immediately:

> May almighty God bless you,
> the Father, and the Son, ✠ and the Holy Spirit.

People: Amen.

or:

B

Prayer over the People

In place of the preceding blessing, the prayer over the people may be used.

The deacon or minister gives the invitation in these or similar words: Bow your heads and pray for God's blessing.

The bishop extends his hands over the people and sings or says:

> God our Father,
> complete the work you have begun
> and keep the gifts of your Holy Spirit
> active in the hearts of your people.
> Make them ready to live his gospel
> and eager to do his will.
> May they never be ashamed
> to proclaim to all the world Christ crucified
> living and reigning for ever and ever.

People: Amen.

The bishop adds immediately:

> **May almighty God bless you,**
> **the Father, and the Son,** ✠ **and the Holy Spirit.**

People: Amen.

RITE OF CONFIRMATION
OUTSIDE MASS

ENTRANCE RITE

34. When the candidates, their sponsors and parents, and the whole assembly of the faithful have gathered, the bishop goes to the sanctuary with the priests who assist him, one or more deacons, and the ministers. Meanwhile all may sing a psalm or appropriate song (see pages 59–64).
35. The bishop makes the usual reverence to the altar with the minister and greets the people:

Bishop: Peace be with you.
People: And also with you.

OPENING PRAYER

Let us pray.
(Prayer in silence)

A
God of power and mercy,
send your Holy Spirit to live in our hearts
and make us temples of his glory.
We ask you this through our Lord Jesus Christ, your Son,
who lives and reigns with you and the Holy Spirit,
one God, for ever and ever. People: Amen.

B
Lord,
fulfill your promise.
Send your Holy Spirit to make us witness before the world
to the Good News proclaimed by Jesus Christ, our Lord,
who lives and reigns with you and the Holy Spirit,
one God, for ever and ever. People: Amen.

C
Lord,
send us your Holy Spirit
to help us walk in unity of faith
and grow in the strength of his love
to the full stature of Christ,
who lives and reigns with you and the Holy Spirit,
one God, for ever and ever. People: Amen.

D
Lord,
fulfill the promise given by your Son
and send the Holy Spirit
to enlighten our minds
and lead us to all truth.

Grant this through our Lord Jesus Christ, your Son, who lives and reigns with you and the Holy Spirit, one God, for ever and ever. People: Amen.

CELEBRATION OF THE WORD OF GOD

36. The celebration of the word of God follows. At least one of the readings suggested for the Mass of confirmation is read. See the readings on pages 48–58.
37. If two or three readings are chosen, the traditional order is followed; that is, the Old Testament, the Apostle, and the Gospel. After the first and second reading there should be a psalm or song, or a period of silence may be observed.

PRESENTATION OF THE CANDIDATES

38. After the readings the bishop (and the priests who assist him) are seated. The pastor or another priest, deacon, or catechist presents the candidates for confirmation according to the custom of the region. If possible, each candidate is called by name and comes individually to the sanctuary. If the candidates are children, they are accompanied by one of their sponsors or parents and both stand before the celebrant.

If there are many candidates, they are not called by name, but take a suitable place before the bishop.

HOMILY OR ADDRESS

39. The bishop then gives a brief homily. He should explain the readings and lead the candidates, their sponsors and parents, and the whole assembly to a deeper understanding of the mystery of confirmation.

He may use these or similar words:

At Pentecost the apostles received the Holy Spirit as the Lord had promised. They also received the power of giving the Holy Spirit and so completing the work of baptism. This we read in the Acts of the Apostles. When Saint Paul placed his hands on those who had been baptized, the Holy Spirit came upon them, and they began to speak in other languages and prophetic words.

Bishops are successors of the apostles and have this power of giving the Holy Spirit to the baptized, either personally or through the priests they appoint.

In our day the coming of the Holy Spirit is not usually marked by the gift of tongues, but we know his coming by faith. He fills our hearts with the love of God, brings us together in one faith but different vocations, and works within us to make the Church one and holy.

The gift of the Holy Spirit which you are to receive will be a spiritual sign and seal to make you more Christ-like and more perfect members of his Church. At his baptism by John, Christ was anointed by the Spirit and sent out on his public ministry to set the world on fire.

You have already been baptized into Christ and now you will receive the power of his Spirit and the sign of the cross on your forehead. You must be witnesses before all the world to his suffering, death, and resurrection; your way of life should reflect the goodness of Christ. Christ gives varied gifts to his Church, and the Spirit distributes them among the members of Christ's body to build up the holy people of God in unity and love.

Be active members of the Church, alive in Jesus Christ. Under the guidance of the Holy Spirit give your lives completely in the service of all, as did Christ, who came not to be served but to serve.

Before you receive the Spirit, renew the profession of faith you made in baptism or your parents and godparents made for you in union with the whole Church.

Renewal of Baptismal Promises

40. *After the homily the candidates stand and the bishop questions them. They respond together.*

Bishop: Do you reject Satan and all his works and all his empty promises?

Candidates: I do.

Bishop: Do you believe in God the Father almighty, creator of heaven and earth?

Candidates: I do.

Bishop: Do you believe in Jesus Christ, his only Son, our Lord, who was born of the Virgin Mary, was crucified, died, and was buried, rose from the dead, and is now seated at the right hand of the Father?

Candidates: I do.

Bishop: Do you believe in the Holy Spirit, the Lord, the giver of life, who came upon the apostles at Pentecost and today is given to you sacramentally in confirmation?

Candidates: I do.

Bishop: Do you believe in the holy catholic Church, the communion of saints, the forgiveness of sins, the resurrection of the body, and life everlasting?

Candidates: I do.

The bishop gives his assent to their profession of faith and proclaims the faith of the Church:

This is our faith. This is the faith of the Church. We are proud to profess it in Christ Jesus our Lord.

The congregation responds:

Amen.

For This is our faith, *some other formula may be substituted, or the community may express its faith in a suitable song (see pages 59-64).*

The Laying on of Hands

The laying of hands on the candidates by the bishop and concelebrating priests expresses the biblical gesture by which the gift of the Holy Spirit is invoked.

41. While the priests who assist the bishop stand near him, he stands facing the people, and with hands joined, sings or says:

My dear friends:
in baptism God our Father gave the new birth of eternal life
to his chosen sons and daughters.
Let us pray to our Father
that he will pour out the Holy Spirit
to strengthen his sons and daughters with his gifts
and anoint them to be more like Christ the Son of God.

All pray in silence for a short time.

42. The bishop and the priests who assist him extend their hands over all the candidates. The bishop alone sings or says:

All-powerful God, Father of our Lord Jesus Christ,
by water and the Holy Spirit
you freed your sons and daughters from sin
and gave them new life.
Send your Holy Spirit upon them
to be their Helper and Guide.
Give them the spirit of wisdom and understanding,
the spirit of right judgment and courage,
the spirit of knowledge and reverence.
Fill them with the spirit of wonder and awe in your presence.
We ask this through Christ our Lord.

People: Amen.

Anointing

Through the anointing with chrism (perfumed oil) the baptized person receives the indelible character, the seal of the Lord, together with the gift of the Spirit which conforms him/her more closely to Christ and gives the grace of spreading the Lord's presence among all people.

43. The deacon brings the chrism to the bishop. Each candidate goes to the bishop, or the bishop may go to the individual candidates. The one who presented the candidate places his/her right hand on the latter's shoulder and gives the candidate's name to the bishop; the candidate, however, may give his/her own name.

44. The bishop dips his right thumb in the chrism and makes the sign of the cross on the forehead of the one to be confirmed as he says:

N., be sealed with the Gift of the Holy Spirit.

The newly-confirmed responds: Amen.

The bishop says: Peace be with you.

The newly-confirmed responds: And also with you.

45. If priests assist the bishop in conferring the sacrament, all the vessels of chrism are brought to the bishop by the deacon or by other ministers. The bishop gives a vessel of chrism to each of the priests.

The candidates go to the bishop or to the priests, or the bishop and priests may go to the candidates. The anointing is done as described above.

46. During the anointing a suitable song may be sung. After the anointing the bishop and the priests wash their hands.

General Intercessions

47. The general intercessions follow, in this or a similar form determined by the competent authority.

Bishop:
My dear friends: let us be one in prayer to God our Father as we are one in the faith, hope, and love his Spirit gives.

Deacon or minister:
For these sons and daughters of God, confirmed by the gift of the Spirit, that they give witness to Christ by lives built on faith and love, let us pray to the Lord:

People: Lord, hear our prayer.

Deacon or minister:
For the newly confirmed, who have received the fullness of God's Spirit, that standing at the altar of the Lord they may share the banquet of Christ's sacrifice, calling God their Father in the midst of the Church, let us pray to the Lord:

People: Lord, hear our prayer.

Deacon or minister:
For the parents and godparents who led them in faith, that by word and example they may always encourage them to follow the way of Jesus Christ, let us pray to the Lord:

People: Lord, hear our prayer.

Deacon or minister:
For the holy Church of God, in union with N. our pope, N. our bishop, and all the bishops, that God, who gathers us together by the Holy Spirit, may help us grow in unity of faith and love until his Son returns in glory, let us pray to the Lord:

People: Lord, hear our prayer.

Deacon or minister:
For all men and women, of every race and nation, that they may acknowledge the one God as Father, and in the bond of common fellowship seek his kingdom, which is peace and joy in the Holy Spirit, let us pray to the Lord:

People: Lord, hear our prayer.

RITE OF CONFIRMATION OUTSIDE MASS

Bishop: God our Father,
you sent the Holy Spirit upon the apostles,
and through them and their successors
you give the Spirit to your people.
May his work begun at Pentecost
continue to grow in the hearts of all who believe.
We ask this through Christ our Lord.

People: Amen.

LORD'S PRAYER

48. All then say the Lord's Prayer, which the bishop may introduce in these or similar words:

Dear friends in Christ,
let us pray together
as the Lord Jesus Christ has taught.

People: Our Father, who art in heaven,
hallowed be thy name;
thy kingdom come;
thy will be done on earth as it
  is in heaven.
Give us this day our daily bread;
and forgive us our trespasses
as we forgive those who trespass against us;
and lead us not into temptation,
but deliver us from evil.

BLESSING

49. After the Lord's Prayer the bishop blesses all present. In place of the usual blessing, the following blessing or prayer over the people is used.

The deacon or minister gives the invitation in these or similar words: Bow your heads and pray for God's blessing.

The bishop extends his hands over the people and sings or says:

God our Father
made you his children by water and the Holy Spirit:
may he bless you
and watch over you with his fatherly love.

People: Amen.

Jesus Christ the Son of God
promised that the Spirit of truth
would be with his Church for ever:
may he bless you and give you courage
in professing the true faith.

People: Amen.

RITE OF CONFIRMATION OUTSIDE MASS

A

> The Holy Spirit
> came down upon the disciples
> and set their hearts on fire with love:
> may he bless you,
> keep you in faith and love
> and bring you to the joy of God's kingdom.

People: Amen.

The bishop adds immediately:

> May almighty God bless you,
> the Father, and the Son, ✠ and the Holy Spirit.

People: Amen.

or:

B

Prayer over the People

In place of the preceding blessing, the prayer over the people may be used.

The deacon or minister gives the invitation in these or similar words: Bow your heads and pray for God's blessing.

The bishop extends his hands over the people and sings or says:

> God our Father,
> complete the work of love you have begun
> and keep the gifts of your Holy Spirit
> active in the hearts of your people.
> Make them ready to live his gospel
> and eager to do his will.
> May they never be ashamed
> to proclaim to all the world Christ crucified
> living and reigning for ever and ever.

People: Amen.

The bishop adds immediately:

> May almighty God bless you,
> the Father, and the Son, ✠ and the Holy Spirit.

People: Amen.

SCRIPTURE READINGS

Any of the following texts may be used in place of the selections given on pages 17–20, or see Lectionary for Mass, nos. 763–767.

OLD TESTAMENT READING

1 Is. 11:1-4

A reading from the book of the prophet Isaiah

On him the Spirit of the Lord rests

A shoot shall sprout from the stump of Jesse,
   and from his roots a bud shall blossom.
The spirit of the Lord shall rest upon him:
   a spirit of wisdom and of understanding,
A spirit of counsel and of strength,
   a spirit of knowledge and of fear of the Lord,
   and his delight shall be the fear of the Lord.
Not by appearance shall he judge,
   nor by hearsay shall he decide,
But he shall judge the poor with justice,
   and decide aright for the land's afflicted.

This is the Word of the Lord.

2 Is. 42:1-3

A reading from the book of the prophet Isaiah

I have endowed my servant with my Spirit

Here is my servant whom I uphold,
   my chosen one with whom I am pleased,
Upon whom I have put my spirit;
   he shall bring forth justice to the nations,
Not crying out, not shouting,
   not making his voice heard in the street.
A bruised reed he shall not break,
   and a smoldering wick he shall not quench.

This is the Word of the Lord.

3 Is. 61:1-3, 6, 8-9

A reading from the book of the prophet Isaiah

*The Lord God has anointed me and has sent me to bring Good News
to the poor, to give them the oil of gladness*

The spirit of the Lord God is upon me,
   because the Lord has anointed me;
He has sent me to bring glad tidings to the lowly,
   to heal the brokenhearted,
To proclaim liberty to the captives
   and release to the prisoners,

To announce a year of favor from the Lord
  and a day of vindication by our God,
  to comfort all who mourn;
To place on those who mourn in Zion
  a diadem instead of ashes.
To give them oil of gladness in place of mourning,
  a glorious mantle instead of a listless spirit.
You yourselves shall be named priests of the Lord,
  ministers of our God you shall be called.
I will give them their recompense faithfully,
  a lasting covenant I will make with them.
Their descendants shall be renowned among the nations,
  and their offspring among the peoples;
All who see them shall acknowledge them
  as a race the Lord has blessed.
                    This is the Word of the Lord.

4   Joel 2:23; 3:1-3

A reading from the book of the prophet Joel

I will pour out my Spirit on all mankind

Do you, O children of Zion, exult
  and rejoice in the Lord, your God!
You shall eat and be filled,
  and shall praise the name of the Lord, your God,
Because he has dealt wondrously with you;
  my people shall nevermore be put to shame.
And you shall know that I am in the midst of Israel;
  I am the Lord, your God, and there is no other;
  my people shall nevermore be put to shame.
Then afterward I will pour out
  my spirit upon all mankind.
Your sons and daughters shall prophesy,
  your old men shall dream dreams,
  your young men shall see visions;
Even upon the servants and the handmaids,
  in those days, I will pour out my spirit.
And I will work wonders in the heavens and on the earth.
                    This is the Word of the Lord.

NEW TESTAMENT READING

1   Acts 1:3-8

A reading from the Acts of the Apostles

You will receive the power of the Holy Spirit, and you will be my witnesses

In the time after his suffering Jesus showed his apostles in many convincing ways that he was alive, appearing to them over the course of forty days and speaking to them about the reign of God. On one occasion when he met with them, he told them not to leave Jerusalem: "Wait, rather, for the fulfillment of my Father's promise, of which you have heard me speak. John baptized with water, but within a few days you will be baptized with the Holy Spirit."

While they were with him they asked, "Lord, are you going to restore the rule to Israel now?"

His answer was: "The exact time it is not yours to know. The Father has reserved that to himself. You will receive power when the Holy Spirit comes down on you; then you are to be my witnesses in Jerusalem, throughout Judea and Samaria, yes, even to the ends of the earth."

This is the Word of the Lord.

2   Acts 2:1-6, 14, 22-23, 32-33

A reading from the Acts of the Apostles

They were all filled with the Holy Spirit, and began to speak

When the day of Pentecost came it found the apostles gathered in one place. Suddenly from up in the sky there came a noise like a strong, driving wind which was heard all through the house where they were seated. Tongues as of fire appeared, which parted and came to rest on each of them. All were filled with the Holy Spirit. They began to express themselves in foreign tongues and make bold proclamation as the Spirit prompted them.

Staying in Jerusalem at the time were devout Jews of every nation under heaven. These heard the sound, and assembled in a large crowd. They were much confused because each one heard these men speaking his own language.

Peter stood up with the Eleven, raised his voice, and addressed them: "You who are Jews, indeed all of you staying in Jerusalem! Listen to what I have to say. Men of Israel, listen to me: Jesus the Nazorean was a man whom God sent to you with miracles, wonders and signs as his credentials. These God worked through him in your midst, as you well know. He was delivered up by the set purpose and plan of God; you even made use of pagans to crucify and kill him. This is the Jesus God has raised up, and we are his witnesses. Exalted at God's right hand, he first received the promised holy Spirit from the Father, then poured this Spirit out on us."

This is the Word of the Lord.

3   Acts 10:1, 33-34, 37-44

A reading from the Acts of the Apostles

The Holy Spirit came down on all those listening to the word of God

In Caesarea there was a centurion named Cornelius, of the Roman cohort Italica, who was religious and God-fearing. The same was true of his whole household.

Cornelius said to Peter: "I sent for you immediately, and you have been kind enough to come. All of us stand before God at this moment to hear whatever directives the Lord has given you."

Peter proceeded to address them in these words: "I take it you know what has been reported all over Judea about Jesus of Nazareth, beginning in Galilee with the baptism John preached; of the way God anointed him with the Holy Spirit and power. He went about doing good works and healing all who were in the grip of the devil, and God was with him. We are witnesses to all that he did in the land of the Jews and in Jerusalem. They killed him finally, 'hanging him on a tree,' only to have God raise him up on the third day and grant that he be seen, not by all, but only by such witnesses as had been chosen beforehand by God — by us who ate and drank with him after he rose from the dead. He commissioned us to preach to the people and to bear witness that he is the one set apart by God as judge of the living and the dead. To him all the prophets testify, saying that everyone who believes in him has forgiveness of sins through his name."

Peter had not finished these words when the Holy Spirit descended upon all who were listening to Peter's message.

This is the Word of the Lord.

4   Acts 19:1-6

A reading from the Acts of the Apostles

Did you receive the Holy Spirit when you became believers?

Paul came to Ephesus. There he found some disciples to whom he put the question, "Did you receive the Holy Spirit when you became believers?"

They answered, "We have not so much as heard that there is a Holy Spirit."

"Well, how were you baptized?" he persisted.

They replied, "With the baptism of John."

Paul then explained, "John's baptism was a baptism of repentance. He used to tell the people about the one who would come after him in whom they were to believe — that is, Jesus." When they heard this, they were baptized in the name of the Lord Jesus. As Paul laid his hands on them, the Holy Spirit came down on them.

This is the Word of the Lord.

5   Rom. 5:1-2, 5-8

A reading from the letter of Paul to the Romans

The love of God has been poured into our hearts by the Holy Spirit which has been given to us

Now that we have been justified by faith, we are at peace with God through our Lord Jesus Christ. Through him we have gained access by faith to the grace in which we now stand, and we boast of our hope for the glory of God. And this hope will not leave us disappointed, because the love of God has been poured out in our hearts through the Holy Spirit who has been given to us. At the appointed time, when we were still powerless, Christ died for us godless men. It is rare that anyone should lay down his life for a just man, though it is barely possible that for a good man someone may have the courage to die. It is precisely in this that God proves his love for us: that while we were still sinners, Christ died for us.

This is the Word of the Lord.

6   Rom. 8:14-17

A reading from the letter of Paul to the Romans

The Spirit himself and our spirit bear united witness that we are children of God

All who are led by the Spirit of God are sons of God. You did not receive a spirit of slavery leading you back into fear, but a spirit of adoption through which we cry out, "Abba!" (that is, "Father"). The Spirit himself gives witness with our spirit that we are children of God. But if we are children, we are heirs as well: heirs of God, heirs with Christ, if only we suffer with him so as to be glorified with him. This is the Word of the Lord.

7 — Rom. 8:26-27
A reading from the letter of Paul to the Romans

The Spirit himself will express our plea in a way that could never be put to words

The Spirit helps us in our weakness, for we do not know how to pray as we ought; but the Spirit himself makes intercession for us with groanings which cannot be expressed in speech. He who searches hearts knows what the Spirit means, for the Spirit intercedes for the saints as God himself wills.

This is the Word of the Lord.

8 — 1 Cor. 12:4-13
A reading from the first letter of Paul to the Corinthians

There is one and the same Spirit giving to each as he wills

There are different gifts but the same Spirit; there are different ministries but the same Lord; there are different works but the same God who accomplishes all of them in everyone. To each person the manifestation of the Spirit is given for the common good. To one the Spirit gives wisdom in discourse, to another the power to express knowledge. Through the Spirit one receives faith; by the same Spirit another is given the gift of healing, and still another miraculous powers. Prophecy is given to one; to another power to distinguish one spirit from another. One receives the gift of tongues, another that of interpreting the tongues. But it is one and the same Spirit who produces all these gifts, distributing them to each as he wills.

The body is one and has many members, but all the members, many though they are, are one body; and so it is with Christ. It was in one Spirit that all of us, whether Jew or Greek, slave or free, were baptized into one body. All of us have been given to drink of the one Spirit.

This is the Word of the Lord.

9 — Gal. 5:16-17, 22-23, 24-25
A reading from the letter of Paul to the Galatians

If we live in the Spirit, let us be directed by the Spirit

Live in accord with the spirit and you will not yield to the cravings of the flesh. The flesh lusts against the spirit and the spirit against the flesh; the two are directly opposed. This is why you do not do what your will intends.

In contrast, the fruit of the spirit is love, joy, peace, patient endurance, kindness, generosity, faith, mildness, and chastity. Those who belong to Christ Jesus have crucified their flesh with its passions and desires. Since we live by the spirit, let us follow the spirit's lead.

This is the Word of the Lord.

10 — Eph. 4:1-6
A reading from the letter of Paul to the Ephesians

There is one body, one Spirit, and one baptism

I plead with you as a prisoner for the Lord, to live a life worthy of the calling you have received, with perfect humility, meekness, and patience, bearing with one another lovingly. Make every effort to preserve the unity which has the Spirit as its origin and peace as its binding force. There is but one body and one Spirit, just as there is but one hope given all of you by your call. There is one Lord, one faith, one baptism; one God and Father of all, who is over all, and works through all, and is in all.

This is the Word of the Lord.

Responsorial Psalm

1   Ps. 22:23-24, 26-27, 28, 31-32

℟. (23) I will proclaim your name to my brothers.

Or: ℟. (John 15:26-27) When the Holy Spirit comes to you, you will be my witness.

All repeat: ℟. I will proclaim your name to my brothers. or When the Holy Spirit comes to you, you will be my witness.

> I will proclaim your name to my brethren;
>> in the midst of the assembly I will praise you:
> "You who fear the Lord, praise him;
>> all you descendants of Jacob, give glory to him."

℟. I will proclaim your name to my brothers. or When the Holy Spirit comes to you, you will be my witness.

> So by your gift will I utter praise in the vast assembly;
>> I will fulfill my vows before those who fear him.
> The lowly shall eat their fill;
>> they who seek the Lord shall praise him:
> "May your hearts be ever merry!"

℟. I will proclaim your name to my brothers. or When the Holy Spirit comes to you, you will be my witness.

> All the ends of the earth
>> shall remember and turn to the Lord;
> All the families of the nations
>> shall bow down before him.
> And to him my soul shall live;
>> my descendants shall serve him.
> Let the coming generation be told of the Lord
>> that they may proclaim to a people yet to be born
>> the justice he has shown.

℟. I will proclaim your name to my brothers. or When the Holy Spirit comes to you, you will be my witness.

2   Ps. 23:1-3, 3-4, 5-6

℟. (1) The Lord is my shepherd; there is nothing I shall want.

All repeat: ℟. The Lord is my shepherd; there is nothing I shall want.

> The Lord is my shepherd; I shall not want.
>> In verdant pastures he gives me repose;
> Beside restful waters he leads me;
>> he refreshes my soul.

℟. The Lord is my shepherd; there is nothing I shall want.

> He guides me in right paths
>> for his name's sake.
> Even though I walk in the dark valley
>> I fear no evil; for you are at my side
> With your rod and your staff
>> that give me courage.

℟. The Lord is my shepherd; there is nothing I shall want.

> You spread the table before me
> > in the sight of my foes;
> You anoint my head with oil;
> > my cup overflows.
> Only goodness and kindness follow me
> > all the days of my life;
> And I shall dwell in the house of the Lord
> > for years to come.

℟. The Lord is my shepherd; there is nothing I shall want.

3   Ps. 96:1-2, 2-3, 9-10, 11-12
℟. (3) Proclaim his marvelous deeds to all the nations.

4   Ps. 117:1, 2
℟. (Acts 1:8) You will be my witnesses to all the world.

5   Ps. 145:2-3, 4-5, 8-9, 10-11, 15-16, 21
℟. (1) I will praise your name for ever, Lord.

Alleluia Verse and Verse before the Gospel

Outside of Lent, the cantor sings Alleluia; it is then repeated by the people. The cantor then sings one of the verses given below, and the people repeat Alleluia.

During Lent, the same pattern is followed, except that one of the following invocations replaces the Alleluia:
(a) Praise to you, Lord Jesus Christ, king of endless glory!
(b) Praise and honor to you, Lord Jesus Christ!
(c) Glory and praise to you, Lord Jesus Christ!
(d) Glory to you, Word of God, Lord Jesus Christ!

1
℣. Alleluia. ℟. Alleluia.   John 14:16
℣. The Father will send you the Holy Spirit, says the Lord,
to be with you for ever. ℟. Alleluia.

2
℣. Alleluia. ℟. Alleluia.   John 15:26, 27
℣. The Spirit of truth will bear witness to me, says the Lord,
and you also will be my witnesses. ℟. Alleluia.

3
℣. Alleluia. ℟. Allelulia.   John 16:33; 14:26
℣. When the Spirit of truth comes, he will teach you all truth
and bring to your mind all I have told you. ℟. Alleluia.

4
℣. Alleluia. ℟. Alleluia.   Rev. 1:5, 6
℣. Jesus Christ, you are the faithful witness, first-born from the dead;
you have made us a kingdom of priests to serve our God and Father.
     ℟. Alleluia.

5
℣. Alleluia. ℟. Alleluia.
℣. Come, Holy Spirit;
shine on us the radiance of your light. ℟. Alleluia.

Gospel

1   Matthew 5:1-12

✠ A reading from the holy gospel according to Matthew

Theirs is the kingdom of heaven

When Jesus saw the crowds he went up on the mountainside. After he had sat down his disciples gathered around him, and he began to teach them: "How blest are the poor in spirit: the reign of God is theirs.
Blest too are the sorrowing; they shall be consoled.
Blest are the lowly; they shall inherit the land.
Blest are they who hunger and thirst for holiness; they shall have their fill.
Blest are they who show mercy; mercy shall be theirs.
Blest are the single-hearted for they shall see God.
Blest too the peacemakers; they shall be called sons of God.
Blest are those persecuted for holiness' sake; the reign of God is theirs.
Blest are you when they insult you and persecute you and utter every kind of slander against you because of me.
Be glad and rejoice, for your reward in heaven is great."

                                                                   This is the gospel of the Lord.

2   Matthew 16:24-27

✠ A reading from the holy gospel according to Matthew

If anyone wishes to follow me, let him deny himself

Jesus said to his disciples: "If a man wishes to come after me, he must deny his very self, take up his cross and begin to follow in my footsteps. Whoever would save his life will lose it, but whoever loses his life for my sake will find it. What profit would a man show if he were to gain the whole world and ruin himself in the process? What can a man offer in exchange for his very self? The Son of Man will come with his Father's glory accompanied by his angels. When he does, he will repay each man according to his conduct."   This is the gospel of the Lord.

3   Matthew 25:14-30

✠ A reading from the holy gospel according to Matthew

Because you have been faithful in small matters, come into the joy of your master

Jesus told this parable to his disciples: "This is the case of a man who was going on a journey. He called in his servants and handed his funds over to them according to each man's abilities. To one he disbursed five thousand silver pieces, to a second two thousand, and to a third a thousand. Then he went away. Immediately the man who received the five thousand went to invest it and made another five. In the same way, the man who received the two thousand doubled his figure. The man who received the thousand went off instead and dug a hole in the ground, where he buried his master's money.

"After a long absence, the master of those servants came home and settled accounts with them. The man who had received the five thousand came forward bringing the additional five. 'My lord,' he said, 'you let me have five thousand. See, I have made five thousand more.'

"His master said to him, 'Well done! You are an industrious and reliable servant. Since you were dependable in a small matter I will put you in charge of larger affairs. Come, share your master's joy!"

"The man who had received the two thousand then stepped forward. 'My lord,' he said, 'you entrusted me with two thousand and I have made two thousand more.'

"His master said to him, 'Cleverly done! You too are an industrious and reliable servant. Since you were dependable in a small matter I will put you in charge of larger affairs. Come, share your master's joy!"

"Finally the man who had received the thousand stepped forward. 'My lord,' he said, 'I knew you were a hard man. You reap where you did not sow and gather where you did not scatter, so out of fear I went off and buried your thousand silver pieces in the ground. Here is your money back.'

"His master exclaimed: 'You worthless, lazy lout! You know I reap where I did not sow and gather where I did not scatter. All the more reason to deposit my money with the bankers, so that on my return I could have had it back with interest. You, there! Take the thousand away from him and give it to the man with the ten thousand. Those who have, will get more until they grow rich, while those who have not, will lose even the little they have. Throw this worthless servant into the darkness outside, where he can wail and grind his teeth.'" This is the gospel of the Lord.

4 Mark 1:9-11

✠ A reading from the holy gospel according to Mark

He saw the Spirit descending and remaining on him

Jesus came from Nazareth in Galilee and was baptized in the Jordan by John. Immediately on coming up out of the water he saw the sky rent in two and the Spirit descending on him like a dove. Then a voice came from the heavens: "You are my beloved Son. On you my favor rests."

This is the gospel of the Lord.

5 Luke 4:16-22

✠ A reading from the holy gospel according to Luke

The Spirit of the Lord is upon me

Jesus came to Nazareth where he had been reared, and entering the synagogue on the sabbath as he was in the habit of doing, he stood up to do the reading. When the book of the prophet Isaiah was handed him, he unrolled the scroll and found the passage where it was written:

"The spirit of the Lord is upon me;
therefore he has anointed me.
He has sent me to bring glad tidings to the poor,
to proclaim liberty to captives,
Recovery of sight to the blind
and release to prisoners,
To announce a year of favor from the Lord."

Rolling up the scroll, he gave it back to the assistant and sat down. All in the synagogue had their eyes fixed on him. Then he began by saying to them, "Today this Scripture passage is fulfilled in your hearing." All who were present spoke favorably of him. This is the gospel of the Lord.

6

✠ A reading from the holy gospel according to Luke

Some seed fell into rich soil. These are the people who receive the word and bear fruit in patience

A large crowd was gathering, with people resorting to Jesus from one town after another. He spoke to them in a parable: "A farmer went out to sow some seed. In the sowing, some fell on the footpath where it was walked on and the birds of the air ate it up. Some fell on rocky ground, sprouted up, then withered through lack of moisture. Some fell among briers, and the thorns growing up with it stifled it. But some fell on good soil, grew up, and yielded grain a hundred-fold."

As he said this he exclaimed: "Let everyone who has ears attend to what he has heard."

His disciples began asking him what the meaning of this parable might be. He replied, "To you the mysteries of the reign of God have been confided. The seed is the word of God. Those on the footpath are people who hear, but the devil comes and takes the word out of their hearts lest they believe and be saved. Those on the rocky ground are the ones who, when they hear the word, receive it with joy. They have no root; they believe for a while, but fall away in time of temptation. The seed fallen among briers are those who hear, but their progress is stifled by the cares and riches and pleasures of life and they do not mature. The seed on good ground are those who hear the word in a spirit of openness, retain it, and bear fruit through perseverance." This is the gospel of the Lord.

7 Luke 10:21-24

✠ A reading from the holy gospel according to Luke

I bless you, Father, for revealing these things to children

Jesus rejoiced in the Holy Spirit and said: "I offer you praise, O Father, Lord of heaven and earth, because what you have hidden from the learned and the clever you have revealed to the merest children.

"Yes, Father, you have graciously willed it so. Everything has been given over to me by my Father. No one knows the Son except the Father and no one knows the Father except the Son — and anyone to whom the Son wishes to reveal him."

Turning to his disciples he said to them privately: "Blest are the eyes that see what you see. I tell you, many prophets and kings wished to see what you see but did not see it, and to hear what you hear but did not hear it."
This is the gospel of the Lord.

8 John 7:37-39

✠ A reading from the holy gospel according to John

From the heart of God shall flow fountains of living water

Jesus stood up and cried out:
"If anyone thirsts, let him come to me;
let him drink who believes in me.
Scripture has it:

'From within him rivers of living water shall flow.'"
(Here he was referring to the Spirit, whom those that came to believe in him were to receive. There was, of course, no Spirit as yet, since Jesus had not yet been glorified.) This is the gospel of the Lord.

9 John 14:15-17

✠ A reading from the holy gospel according to John

The spirit of truth will be with you for ever

Jesus said to his disciples:
"If you love me
and obey the commands I give you,
I will ask the Father
and he will give you another Paraclete —
to be with you always:
the Spirit of truth,
whom the world cannot accept,
since it neither sees him nor recognizes him;
but you can recognize him
because he remains with you
and will be within you."

This is the gospel of the Lord.

10 John 15:18-21, 26-27

✠ A reading from the holy gospel according to John

The Spirit of truth, who issues from the Father, will be my witness

Jesus said to his disciples:
"If you find that the world hates you,
know it has hated me before you.
If you belonged to the world,
it would love you as its own;
the reason it hates you
is that you do not belong to the world.
But I chose you out of the world.
Remember what I told you:
no slave is greater than his master.
They will harry you
as they harried me.
They will respect your words
as much as they respected mine.
All this they will do to you because of my name,
for they know nothing of him who sent me.
When the Paraclete comes,
the Spirit of truth who comes from the Father —
and whom I myself will send from the Father —
he will bear witness on my behalf.
You must bear witness as well,
for you have been with me from the beginning."

This is the gospel of the Lord.

8. WITH JOYFUL HEARTS WE ENTER

With joy-ful hearts we en-ter the ho-ly place of God.

1. May your faith - ful - ness and jus - tice   draw us
2. Let   us praise our God and Sav - ior   who re-
3. Let   us   of - fer there to - geth - er   God's own
4. Glo - ry   be   to   God the Fa - ther, glo - ry

1. to your ho - ly al - tar, There the sac - ri - fice to
2. news our joy in liv - ing As we near the ho - ly
3. Son, the sav - ing vic - tim, Who by dy - ing makes us
4. be to Christ our lead - er; And to God the Ho - ly

1. of - fer which to   you gives bound - less glo - ry.
2. moun - tain where God gives his life to save us.
3. shar - ers in his light and life e - ter - nal.
4. Spir - it praise be giv - en with - out end - ing.

9. ON THIS DAY, THE FIRST OF DAYS   *Org. Acc. 16*

1. On this day, the first of days, God the Father's name we praise.
   Who, creation's Lord and spring, did the world from darkness bring.

2. On this day th'eternal Son over death his triumph won.
   On this day the Spirit came with his gifts of living flame.

3. Word made flesh, all hail to Thee, thou from sin has set us free:
   And with Thee we die and rise, unto God in sacrifice.

4. Holy Spirit, you impart, gifts of love to ev'ry heart:
   Give us light and grace, we pray, fill our hearts this holy day.

10. PRAISE TO THE LORD

Praise to the Lord, the Almighty, the King of creation!   *Org. Acc. 1*
O my soul, praise him for he is our health and salvation.
All you who hear now to his presence draw near;
Join in profound adoration.
Praise to the Lord, let us offer our gifts at the altar.
Let not our sins and offenses now cause us to falter.
Christ, the High Priest, bids us all join in his feast,
Victims with him on the altar.
Praise to the Lord, O let all that is in us adore him.
All that has life and breath come now rejoicing before him.
Let the Amen sound from his people again,
As we here worship before him.

11. WE ARE HIS PEOPLE

Org. Acc. 376

We are his people: the sheep of his flock.

1. Sing joyfully to the Lord, all you lands;
   serve the Lord with gladness;
   come before him with joyful song.
2. Know that the Lord is God;
   he made us, his we are;
   his people, the flock he tends.
3. The Lord is good:
   his kindness endures for ever,
   and his faithfulness, to all generations.

12. ALLELUIA

Org. Acc. 395

℣. Alleluia. *All repeat* Alleluia.

℣. Your words, O Lord, are spirit and life, you have the  words of everlasting life. *All repeat* Alleluia.

13. FAITH OF OUR FATHERS

Org. Acc. 175

Faith of our fathers! living still
In spite of dungeon, fire, and sword;
Oh how our hearts beat high with joy
When e'er we hear that glorious word:

Faith of our fathers! Mary's prayers
Shall win our country unto thee;
And through the truth that comes from God
Our people shall be truly free:

Refrain: Faith of our fathers, holy faith We will be true to thee till death.

16. CREATOR SPIRIT ALL DIVINE

Org. Acc. 114

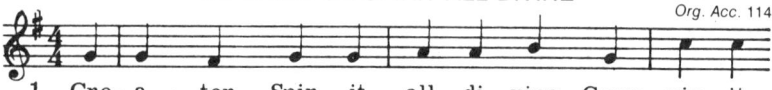

1. Cre-a-tor Spir-it all di-vine, Come vis-it
2. O gift of God, thine is the sweet Con-sol-ing
3. To us, through thee, the grace be shown To know the

1. ev-'ry soul of thine And fill with thy ce-
2. name of Par-a-clete, Thou spring of life and
3. Fa-ther and the Son; And Spir-it of them

1. les-tial flame The hearts which thou thy-self did frame.
2. fire of love And sav-ing unc-tion from a-bove.
3. both, may we For-ev-er rest our faith in thee.

17. COME, HOLY GHOST, CREATOR BLEST

Org. Acc. 450

Come, Holy Ghost, Creator blest,
And in our hearts take up thy rest;
Come with thy grace and heav'nly aid
To fill the hearts which thou hast made.

O Comforter, to thee we cry,
Thou gift of God sent from on high,
Thou font of life and fire of love,
The soul's anointing from above.

Make thou to us the Father known,
Through thee his Son in faith be shown;
Be this our never changing creed:
That thou dost from them both proceed.

To God the Father let us sing,
To God the Son our risen King,
And equally let us adore
The Spirit, God for evermore.

18. COME, HOLY SPIRIT, GOD-HEAD ONE

Org. Acc. 113

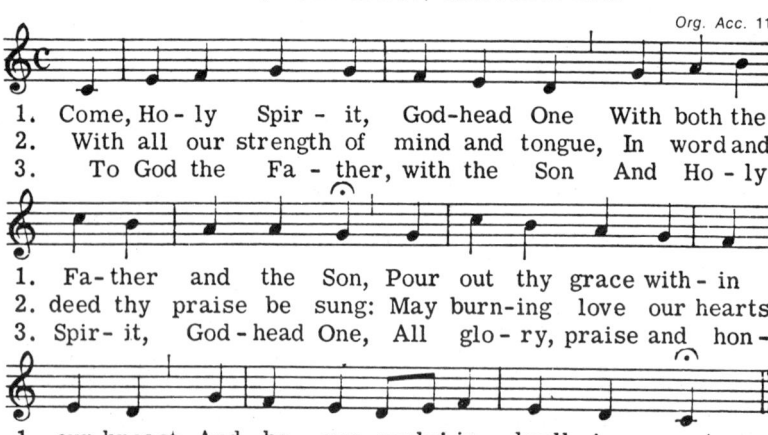

1. Come, Ho-ly Spir-it, God-head One With both the
2. With all our strength of mind and tongue, In word and
3. To God the Fa-ther, with the Son And Ho-ly

1. Fa-ther and the Son, Pour out thy grace with-in
2. deed thy praise be sung: May burn-ing love our hearts
3. Spir-it, God-head One, All glo-ry, praise and hon-

1. our breast, And be our souls' in-dwell-ing guest.
2. in-spire, In-flam-ing oth-ers with its fire.
3. or be, In time and in e-ter-ni-ty.

19. GIFT OF FINEST WHEAT

Omer Westendorf
86. 86.D. with refrain
Robert E. Kreutz
Or. Acc. 512

REFRAIN
You satisfy the hungry heart With gift of finest wheat; Come give to us, O saving Lord, The bread of life to eat.

1. As when the shepherd calls his sheep, They know and heed his voice; So when you call your fam-'ly, Lord, We follow and rejoice.
2. With joyful lips we sing to you Our praise and gratitude, That you should count us worthy, Lord, To share this heav'n-ly food.
3. Is not the cup we bless and share The blood of Christ outpoured? Do not one cup, one loaf, declare Our oneness in the Lord?
4. The mys-t'ry of your presence, Lord, No mortal tongue can tell: Whom all the world cannot contain Comes in our hearts to dwell.
5. You give yourself to us, O Lord; Then selfless let us be, To serve each other in your name In truth and char-i-ty.

© 1976, Board of Governors, 41st International Eucharistic Congress, Inc.

20. PEACE PRAYER OF ST. FRANCIS

Org. Acc. 533
Sebastian Temple

Make me a channel of your peace.
Where there is hatred, let me bring your love.
Where there is injury, your pardon, Lord.
And where there's doubt, true faith in you.

Make me a channel of your peace.
Where there's despair in life, let me bring hope.
Where there is darkness only light.
And where there's sadness ever joy.

O Master, grant that I may never seek.
So much to be consoled as to console.
To be understood as to understand.
To be loved, as to love, with all my soul.

Make me a channel of your peace.
It is in pardoning that we are pardoned.
In giving of ourselves that we receive.
And in dying that we're born to eternal life.

©1967 Franciscan Communications Center

21. JOYFUL, JOYFUL WE ADORE THEE

Org. Acc. 150 or 588

1. Joyful, joyful we adore thee, God of glory, Lord of love.
   Hearts unfold like flow'rs before thee, praising thee, their Sun above.
   Melt the clouds of sin and sadness, drive the dark of doubt away.
   Giver of immortal gladness, fill us with the light of day.

2. All thy works with joy surround thee, earth and heav'n reflect thy rays.
   Stars and angels sing around thee, center of unbroken praise.
   Field and forest, vale and mountain, flow'ry meadow, flashing sea.
   Chanting bird and flowing fountain, call us to rejoice in thee.

3. Thou art giving and forgiving, ever blessing, ever blest.
   Well spring of the joy of living, ocean depth of happy rest!
   Thou our Father, Christ our Brother, all who live in love are thine.
   Teach us how to love each other, lift us to the joy divine.

4. Mortals, join in the mighty chorus which the morning stars began.
   Father love is reigning o'er us, brother love binds man to man.
   Ever singing, march we onward, victors in the midst of strife.
   Joyful music lifts us sunward in the triumph song of life.

22. O GOD, ALMIGHTY FATHER

Org. Acc. 46

O God, almighty Father, Creator of all things,
The heavens stand in wonder, while earth thy glory sings.

Refrain: O most holy Trinity, undivided Unity;
          Holy God, mighty God, God immortal, be adored!

O Jesus, Word incarnate, Redeemer most adored,
All glory, praise and honor be thine, our sov'reign Lord.

O God, the Holy Spirit, who lives within our soul,
Send forth thy light and lead us to our eternal goal.

23. HOLY GOD, WE PRAISE THY NAME

Org. Acc. 59

1. Holy God, we praise thy name! Lord of all, we bow before thee!
   All on earth thy sceptre 'claim,[1] All in heaven above adore thee.
   Infinite thy vast domain, Everlasting is thy reign!

2. Hark, the loud celestial hymn angel choirs above are raising!
   Cherubim and Seraphim, in unceasing chorus praising,
   Fill the heavens with sweet accord; holy, holy, holy Lord!

3. Holy Father, Holy Son! Holy Spirit, Three we name thee,
   While in essence only One, Undivided God we 'claim thee;
   And adoring bend the knee, While we own the mystery.

Abbreviated from: acclaim.

24. I SING THE MIGHTY POWER OF GOD

Org. Acc. 155

I sing the mighty power of God, that made the mountains rise.
That spread the flowing seas abroad, and built the lofty skies.
I sing the wisdom that ordained the sun to rule the day.
The moon shines full at his command, and all the stars obey.

I sing the goodness of the Lord, that filled the earth with food.
He formed the creatures with his word, and then pronounced them good.
Lord, how thy wonders are displayed, where'er I turn my eye.
If I survey the ground I tread, or gaze upon the sky!